IN THE SHADOW OF
FUJISAN

IN THE SHADOW OF
FUJISAN

JAPAN
AND ITS WILDLIFE

by
JO STEWART-SMITH

With photographs by
SIMON McBRIDE

VIKING/RAINBIRD

VIKING

Penguin Books Ltd, Harmondsworth, Middlesex, England
Viking Penguin Inc., 40 West 23rd Street, New York, New York 10010, U.S.A.
Penguin Books Australia Ltd, Ringwood, Victoria, Australia
Penguin Books Canada Limited, 2801 John Street, Markham, Ontario, Canada L3R 1B4
Penguin Books (N.Z.) Ltd, 182–190 Wairau Road, Auckland 10, New Zealand

First published 1987

Text copyright © The Moving Picture Company Ltd 1987

Photographs by Simon McBride
copyright © The Rainbird Publishing Group Ltd 1987

This book was designed and produced by
The Rainbird Publishing Group Ltd
27 Wrights Lane
London W8 5TZ

Text set by Goodfellow & Egan, Cambridge
Colour origination by Anglia Graphics, Bedford
Printed and bound by Hazell, Watson & Viney Ltd., Aylesbury

Designed by Lester Cheeseman

British Library Cataloguing in Publication Data

Stewart-Smith, Jo
In the Shadow of Fujisan.
1. Natural history – Japan
I. Title
574.952   QH188
ISBN 0-670-81789-9

Opposite title page: *Cherry trees in the
Kenrokuen gardens in Kanazawa. The falling
blossoms symbolize all that is ephemeral in Japan.*

Facing page: *Infant Japanese macaques grow up
in the protective care of the troop.*

CONTENTS

INTRODUCTION

Fujisan, rising up out of the coastal plains, dominates a huge area of land southwest of Tokyo. Her summit seems to hang in the horizon of the sky – a sacred mountain, the eternal symbol of Japan. In ancient lore the mountain rose when the year of the monkey coincided with the year of the wood. The whole of Fujisan from the forests at her base to the tip of her crater is a sacred *kami* or spirit, and volcanic summits all over Japan are named after her. For many she embodies the ultimate beauty of Japan.

Today Fujisan is dormant but her power lies in her intransigence, her temperamental mood: if you blink she may vanish in the mist. Disorientated, you search in vain, then suddenly she reappears. As you get closer Fujisan is suddenly small; worse, she appears vulnerable. She has a bite out of one side and it is feared that further erosion will cause the loss of her symmetrical shape. Pylons and telegraph poles festoon her. If you want to retain an image of powerful Fujisan, this is the time to turn back. If you continue towards the summit you may find, as I did, that her wild beauty lies tarnished.

Like her favourite mountain Japan presents a huge paradox to westerners. Ask a Japanese about the Japanese attitude to wildlife and you unlock a tantalizing picture – of the pilgrimages to see cherry blossoms in spring and the seven grasses of autumn, of the reverence for wild nature inherent in Shinto, the flow of

Facing page: Fujisan, the sacred mountain, her symmetry reflected in the still waters of Lake Kawaguchi. In a land where anything which evoked awe became a kami, *Fujisan reigned supreme.*

Right: *Fujisan from a* pachinko *parlour.* Pachinko *or pinball is a favourite national pastime. The Fuji-Hakone-Izu National Park, a popular tourist area, must meet the demand.*

nature in a Zen-inspired garden, the mirroring of the passing of the seasons in the home; of the evocative symbolism of cranes and pines or wild geese and the moon; of nature reflected in poetry, songs, paintings and dances. Above all, one senses the oneness of the Japanese with nature, closer they say than those in the West, where Christianity has set man above and apart from wildlife. Yet, despite these glimpses of a passionate attachment to nature, Japan has a poor international reputation with regard to conserving her wildlife and habitats. Conservationists also accuse her of fostering much of the world trade in endangered species like sea-turtles, crocodiles, primates, musk deer and tropical hardwoods and of continuing to whale after most other nations have stopped.

The Japanese are fully aware that whaling is unpopular. They say in their defence that far more red meat is eaten by western nations which eat not only domestic animals but also deer, rabbit and game birds. Meat eating in Japan, as a rule, was forbidden after Buddhism became established in the sixth century; hence the traditional vegetarian and seafood diet. The whale was considered to be a fish and the written character meaning whale is built up from one which reads fish; even today whale is sold by the fishmonger, not the butcher. A number of city people were shocked at the thought of westerners eating such a lovable creature as the rabbit. In Japan there is a rabbit rather than a man in the moon and every autumn sweet rice cakes and dumplings are presented to the moon and the rabbit. It is a question of culture.

Since the Second World War Japan has achieved an economic miracle and become one of the world's great trading nations. It therefore comes as a surprise to many westerners to discover that the man with whom they have done business might still use oriental medicine, participate in a monkey-chasing festival or refuse to allow his daughter to marry into a 'fox-owning family'. As a leading influence in Asia, Japan cannot be ignored – her attitude to wildlife over the next few years could be crucial to conservation.

One image of Japan, spread by the foreigner who visits only Tokyo, is that in attaining her goal of economic and technological achievement, she has not allowed anything, including wildlife, to stand in her way. Visitors often return with false reports that there is barely a blade of grass, let alone any wild animals or birds to be seen. In fact Japan, once attached to the Eurasian continent, and only partly affected by the ice age, has an abundance of species: 130 mammals, over 500 different birds, 50 amphibians, 76 reptiles and around 100,000 species of insects.

A belief that a rabbit pounding rice can be seen in the full moon provides the inspiration for Keigaku's print entitled 'The hares in the moon preparing the elixir of life'. (By courtesy of the Board of Trustees of the Victoria & Albert Museum)

Roughly 66 per cent of the mammals are endemic, species found nowhere else but Japan. The variety of species is explained partly by the variety of landscape and habitat. More than 3,800 islands are clustered around the main islands of Hokkaido, Honshu, Shikoku and Kyushu which describe a long, shallow curve. The islands stretch from the Sea of Okhotsk, which laps against Russia, nearly 2,800 km southwest to the Ryukyu Islands which almost reach Taiwan.

Ranging from a latitude of 45° in the north to 21° in the south, the climate graduates from subarctic to subtropical. Forests once covered 90 per cent of the land and still support over 6,000 plant species. In Hokkaido the natural forest is mostly coniferous; northeast Japan is dominated by deciduous broad-leaved woodland, predominantly beech, with some oak, birch and chestnut; while the southwest is characterized by broad-leaved evergreen forests. At the southern tip of Japan, in the semi-tropical Ryukyu

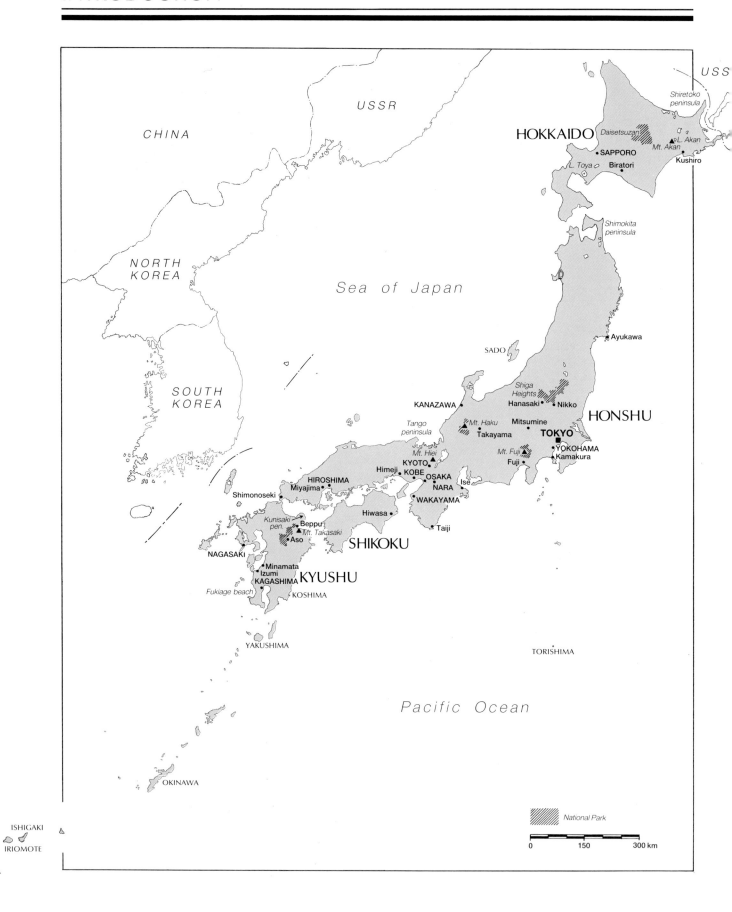

USSR

CHINA

USSR

Shiretoko peninsula

HOKKAIDO

Daisetsuzan • L. Akan

▲ Mt. Akan

• SAPPORO

L. Toya • Biratori

Kushiro

Shimokita peninsula

NORTH KOREA

Sea of Japan

• Ayukawa

SOUTH KOREA

SADO

Shiga Heights

KANAZAWA

Hanasaki • Nikko

HONSHU

Tango peninsula

▲ *Mt. Haku* Mitsumine

• Takayama

TOKYO

Mt. Hiei ▲

Mt. Fuji ▲ YOKOHAMA

KYOTO • Fuji • Kamakura

Himeji • KOBE

HIROSHIMA OSAKA

Miyajima • NARA Ise

Shimonoseki • WAKAYAMA

Kunisaki pen. Beppu Hiwasa

▲ *Mt. Takasaki* • Taiji

Aso SHIKOKU

NAGASAKI

• Minamata

Izumi

KAGASHIMA KYUSHU

Fukiage beach • KOSHIMA

YAKUSHIMA

TORISHIMA

Pacific Ocean

OKINAWA

National Park

0   150   300 km

ISHIGAKI

IRIOMOTE

The Doro gorge in Wakayama prefecture. In Japan's varied and undulating landscape every twist of the road yields a new view.

Islands, tree ferns, pandanas and mangroves grow. Japan's backbone of mountain ranges adds more variation to this pattern. Rising sharply from the plains, they are cut through by deep gorges and softened by valleys, lakes and alpine meadows. Heavy rain and snowfall on the western coast also influences the vegetation.

Japan's mountain ranges are relatively young. Much of the landmass was formed around 20 million years ago and Japan finally separated from the continent more than a million years ago. Japan lies on a ring of fire, an axis of volcanic activity caused by the Eurasian plate rubbing against the Pacific plate, deep in the sea bed. Much of the archipelago is still restless. All over Japan I saw ponds of bubbling mud, yellow sulphur spitting and steaming from rock fissures and brightly coloured red and blue mineral pools. I bathed in hot springs, many of which now have hotels built around them. In southeast Hokkaido on clear days a white plume drifts upwards from Me-Akandake; the crater lakes in this area are among the deepest and most beautiful in the world.

INTRODUCTION

*Hot **bokke** or bubbling mud pools in Akan National Park. The bubbles form, grow and then burst, sending a fountain of mud high into the air.*

In the west of Hokkaido white steam rises daily from the dome-shaped Showa Shinzan, which burst from the side of Mount Usu in 1944. In 1977 Usu erupted again. Eight years later I climbed to the mouth of the new crater on a ghostly day when the swirling mist mingled with the rising steam. Trudging through an eerie forest of naked trunks and over a vast area of undulating thick black ash, I thought that at any moment I might slide down a black river into the mouth of the volcano. Even in this grey moonscape there were signs that life was returning. A snow hare, white against the black, galloped up a rise attracting the attention of three birds of prey. Mammal footprints were easy to spot, a fox loped through the dead forest and woodpeckers hammered at the trees. Many kilometres south, in Kyushu, I looked down into the awesome 20-km diameter Aso caldera. On the day I visited Kagoshima, the volcano Sakurajima (cherry blossom isle) was hidden behind its own angry black soot. As her abundant volcanic activity is relatively recent, however, Japan's wealth has not been built on mineral resources; for hundreds of years her economy was based on rice cultivation.

*   *   *

Facing page: All that is left of a forest after Mount Usu in southwest Hokkaido erupted in 1977. Even here I heard woodpeckers tapping the dead tree trunks; plants and animals quickly recolonize devastated land.

The official date for the founding of the Japanese empire is 660 BC, though historians generally suggest that the first emperor, Emperor Jimmu, reigned in the first century AD. By the sixth century AD the Yamato family had unified most of central Japan and the imperial line remains unbroken. The earliest written records of the founding of Japan were not compiled

until the eighth century, but archaeological studies have shown that during the Jōmon period, from around 8000 to 300 BC, the archipelago was colonized by a people who hunted and gathered using stone implements. From around 300 BC the Yayoi culture, which displaced or absorbed that of the Jōmon people, appeared, spreading the technique of wet rice agriculture over the islands. As farming techniques became more sophisticated, methods for cultivating other crops such as mulberry for silk worms and soya bean were gradually implemented and bamboo, cedar and cypress were planted. Rice paddies have to be flat to hold water. But only about 20 per cent of Japan was naturally flat so, having cleared the lowland flora, the farmers began to terrace the hills. Used to eruptions, earthquakes, typhoons and tidal waves changing the face of the land, the early rice farmers moved huge quantities of earth to create land suitable for cultivation. Westerners are often dismayed to discover the ease and frequency with which the Japanese continue to move whole mountains to provide earthfill or create space, drastically altering the shape of their countryside. But they have been doing so for two thousand years. Modern machinery has simply speeded up the process. Land for development is at a premium and this has a profound effect on the Japanese ability to give space to nature.

A terraced hillside in Nagasaki prefecture on Kyushu Island – history in a landscape. With the arrival of rice in 300 BC the valleys were planted, then the hills were terraced and in this century the higher reaches have been planted with conifers to create a colourful mix, vibrant and busy to the eye.

The lack of land has meant that the Japanese are one of the few cultures that have traditionally never raised or herded livestock. Even today the cows that graze on the fertile volcanic plains to be found near Aso in Kyushu or in Hokkaido are tourist attractions.

One factor affecting land distribution is that over her formative years Japan had a strong class system. While the emperors lived in the capital along with their attendant priests, scholars and warriors, the economy depended on the people in the provinces. The class system evolved gradually as people of different clans were conquered. At the bottom of the scale were the peasants who worked the land. They were crippled by heavy taxes, some of them being no better off than land slaves, and they had no choice but to give their allegiance to the local landowners. The rulers granted favours to friendly clan leaders in the form of land and tax exemptions thus accentuating class divisions. Through the Nara and the Heian periods the court aristocrats had time to admire the cherry blossom and autumn leaves while the farmers fought to keep wild nature away from their crops. The age of the shoguns did little to change the class system and it was not until the Meiji restoration in 1868, when Japan opened her doors to western thought and technology, that opportunities for the land labourers improved. After the Second World War the emperor renounced his divine leadership and Japan officially became a democracy. Many of the huge estates were given back to the people. But in war-torn Japan the cities attracted the people away from the countryside.

Today most of Japan's 120 million people are crowded into only 3 per cent of the land area – the flat river valleys, coastal areas and open plains, such as the Kanto plain around Tokyo. As much as 80 per cent of the population lives in urban areas. The majority, having left the country during the last thirty years, acknowledge their origins and return home for seasonal festivals. Yet I met more than one businessman who remembers with a shudder having to plant rice by hand as a child.

Despite the fact that Japan is now the third most successful industrial nation in the world, it is still possible to find pockets of traditional farmland or natural habitats. In the central islands the forested plains have long been displaced, initially by rice but increasingly by sprawling cities and big industry. But in the valleys and hills neat rice paddies and terraces climb to clumps of bamboo or fruit trees. Soya and radishes are grown in any space that can be found and even the edges of the paddies are planted with onions and other vegetables. The scene is topped with dark conifer plantations. The houses are scattered, creating

Lake Kawaguchi near Fujisan. The rain has washed away the colour in the landscape, creating an ethereal scene that is more like an ink painting than a photograph.

a mix, vibrant and busy to the eye, with every last scrap of land put to use. In the distance, sometimes etched sharply, at other times an ink wash, obscure in the haze or mysterious in the mist, are the mountain ranges. Rising to 3,000 m, well above the treeline, much of this area is still wild, inaccessible and rich with wildlife. The Japanese macaque or monkey lives in the mountain forests with the black bears, the kamoshika or serow, the racoon dog, birds of prey and sika deer.

The northern island of Hokkaido is different from the rest of Japan, a more restful landscape with its sparser conifer forests, high mountain ranges, open grassy spaces and salmon rivers. Its fields, houses and farms are on a much larger scale and cattle and wheat rather than rice dominate. A biological divide known as Blakiston's Line runs across the sea barrier between Hokkaido and Honshu separating the fauna of Hokkaido from the rest of Japan. Blakiston's fishowl is found there as is the Ezo fox, a different sub-species from the fox in Honshu. The fauna of Hokkaido is more closely related to that of Siberia than to that of the rest of Japan. Thus there is a brown instead of a black bear, the Hokkaido squirrel, the Siberian chipmunk and the Asiatic pika, as well as breeding Siberian rubythroats, red-necked grebes and hazel grouse. In autumn whooper swans and large flocks of white-fronted and bean geese pass through. Hokkaido is also home to the red-crowned crane.

While Hokkaido and northeast Honshu are blanketed by heavy snow through the winter, snow rarely reaches the southern island of Kyushu. Here, where huge flocks of migrant hooded and white-naped cranes overwinter, planted palm trees flourish, sea-turtles breed on the beaches and the vegetation is a richer, lusher tangle. The Ryukyu Islands with their white

Lake Akan in southeast Hokkaido with the dormant volcanic cone of O-Akan. The caldera lake is home to the marimo, a unique species of floating alga (see page 32). With much of the ancient forest still standing, this region of mountains, lakes and valleys is rich in wildlife.

beaches, turquoise clear waters, luxuriant forests and mangrove-fringed rivers are truly semi-tropical. Birds from the tropics such as the crested serpent-eagle and the emerald dove are found here at the edge of their breeding range. The fauna and flora are exotic and often unique to just one of the islands. The Ryukyus have been called the Galapagos of the orient and new species are still being discovered there. In 1965 a primitive wildcat known as the Iriomote cat excited the scientific world, in 1981 the Okinawa rail was first described and in 1983 a new species of beetle was discovered.

The seas of Japan, as rich in variety as her land, provide a plentiful harvest. Seals, sharks, sea-snakes, many species of whale, dolphin and sea-turtle live in the coastal waters together with horseshoe crabs, relatives of the ancient fossil tribolites, and the giant spider crab whose legs have a 3-metre span. The seas around the Ryukyu Islands teem with the colourful life of the coral reef community. The battering of the west coast by the Sea of Japan has fashioned strange rock formations, while the Pacific east coast is blessed with the warmer, more benevolent Black Current. On the cold northern shores of Hokkaido the fishermen are kept busy until the sea-ice in the Okhotsk locks hard against the land.

At Shiretoko peninsula in northeast Hokkaido the sea-eagles arrive in November, when the ice prevents them from feeding in their northern fishing grounds, and migrate back across the cape towards the Kurile Islands around the end of February. At

Mangrove forest on Iriomote, one of the southernmost semi-tropical Ryukyu Islands. Mangroves have air-breathing roots as the waterlogged soil does not provide the tree with enough oxygen. Some of the mangroves have an unusual method of reproduction: the seed germinates while still inside the fruit; roots pierce the fruit wall and continue to grow before the new plant drops off.

The Hashi gui rocks off the tip of the peninsula south of Taiji in Wakayama prefecture stretch out to sea like a line of pilgrims.

night they roost in the tree-clad cliffs. Up at 5 a.m. to see the eagles, shivering in the night air at −20°C, I wondered why I had not stayed on my warm *futon*. Then the first dark shapes drifted across the stars. Out to sea an orange line grew bright and gradually lit the distant islands blue-black against a rainbow dawn. The fishing fleet, lights winking, followed the ice-breaking boat as it weaved a path through the sea-ice. The sickle moon grew dim as the sky turned red, then pink, and finally a strong turquoise blue. By 6 a.m. the count had reached over four hundred eagles – it is thought that as many as two and a half thousand eagles winter in this peninsula. Used to scanning the Scottish skies for one lone eagle, it was wonderful to see so many streaming seawards out from the cliffs. Against the blue sky and the black of their bodies, the white shoulder of the Steller's sea-eagle clearly stood out, its size and shape distinguishing it from the smaller white-tailed eagle. It was exhilarating to watch as they soared and flapped with bright orange beaks and neatly tucked yellow feet. I wandered down to the shore to see if I could spot the eagles, far out, fishing, or

Winter lasts for six months in the Shiretoko peninsula in northeast Hokkaido. Ice floes drifting in the Sea of Okhotsk force the seaduck – scoters, goldeneye, scaup and mergansers – to feed in the narrow channels of water close against the shore and in the heart of winter the ice will lock hard against the land.

A Steller's sea-eagle coming in to land at Shiretoko peninsula. At dawn hundreds of eagles stream out from the tree-clad cliffs to hunt amid the ice floes. With their 2.5m wingspan, the sea-eagles are a magnificent sight.

perching on the ice floes amongst the seals and Steller's sea-lions. A pair of mergansers fed in the river and in the bay, squeezed close to the shore by the ice, was a raft of scoters, harlequin and long-tailed ducks. Pelagic cormorants flew out to sea and goldeneye chortled and chucked their heads in a courtship display.

I visited the four major islands and a number of the smaller ones including the Ryukyus and was shown a huge variety of areas and habitats by over a hundred different naturalists and local people. I remember gliding through the mangrove forests of Iriomote by boat to catch a glimpse of the elusive Iriomote cat or the crested serpent-eagle fishing for water-snakes. Walking through the jungle towards a waterfall I found bougainvillea, hibiscus and the huge plate-like roots of the looking-glass tree. In Hakusan National Park a golden eagle soared overhead and Japanese serows ploughed through the snow on the steep slopes. I watched entranced as an Ainu sculptor deftly carved a log into a fishowl and as the shrine maidens danced the delicate butterfly dance.

I remember too the schoolchildren who counted the cranes in Hokkaido and rescued turtle eggs in Shikoku and the student group dedicated to saving the serow with whom I shared rice balls and pickled mushrooms in the mountains as they questioned me about conservation in England. I remember the

*A butterfly dancer, her costume and style of dance, known as **bugaku**, heavily influenced by Chinese culture. The butterfly dance is one of many named after insects, birds and flowers.*

first glimpse of Hiyoshi shrine, the red *torii* or arch peeping through the green cedars. I recall the red of the 'blood pool' at Beppu, contrasting with the green of the overhanging pine tree and the red soil of Okinawa eroding and seeping into the coral sea. The most searing memory I have was of rounding a cove to be confronted by the blood of slaughtered dolphins freshly spilling in a slick across the green sea. One cannot ignore the shadow.

It is virtually impossible to escape the scars and signs of development in Japan. Everywhere forests are being felled, roads pushed across rugged terrain, mountains gouged or flattened; hotels, viewing sites, cable cars and all the garish trappings of tourism erected. Travelling though eighteen of the twenty-seven national parks (which cover 5.4 per cent of the country) I found some of Japan's famous scenic beauty but I was also shocked by the scale of the development. Fujisan is within a national park and from spring to autumn one can pay a toll and drive up to the fifth station, two-thirds of the way up the mountain. There is a huge parking area with shops, restaurants, horses to ride and photographers. Coachloads arrive, crowds emerge and immediately line up to have their photographs taken. At the shops they can buy miniature replicas of Fujisan and bottles selling 'pure canned air'.

When I visited Fujisan the top of the mountain was closed by snow but during July and August pilgrims, following an ancient tradition, still climb through the night arriving at the summit to greet the sunrise. I wondered whether the spirit of Fujisan was rekindled when one climbed her. But the summit is only five hours from the fifth station and I was told that when the sun lights Fujisan it reveals the tin cans and other rubbish left behind by the visitors who had come to see Japan's symbol of ultimate purity.

All over Japan I met people who were concerned about the loss of so much of their country's natural beauty. The television films we were making gave me a unique opportunity to meet and ask questions of fishermen, priests, artists, whalers, and many of those whose work involves trading or using the products of endangered species as well as local people who were trying to protect wildlife or habitat. The opinions of the Japanese about their attitude to wildlife are as varied as their countryside. In order to progress beyond the common misconception that whaling typifies the Japanese approach to wildlife I must start at the beginning and look at the lifestyle of the early peoples who inhabited the islands and also examine the influence of the two major religions, Shinto and Buddhism.

1

THE GODS OF PROMISE

The snail
Wearing a camellia
For a hat.

A late seventeenth-century poem by Sakagami Jinshirō

The origins of the Japanese people and their early beliefs are lost in history but archaeological evidence suggests that the islands were first occupied by the Jōmon people who were hunters and gatherers. The descendants of a people known as the Ainu still live in Hokkaido. Where they came from and whether they are related to the Jōmon people is in dispute. It is thought that the Jōmon culture gradually disappeared as rice cultivation spread from about 300 BC. The first mention of a race generally assumed to be the Ainu appears in the early records of Japanese history from the Nara and Heian periods when Japanese armies were kept busy fighting a people from the north. The Ainu were also hunters and gatherers and traces of Ainu language suggest that they once lived over much of northeast Japan. By the end of the Heian period most Ainu had probably either integrated with the Japanese or were living in Hokkaido.

In a recent survey about 24,000 people from Hokkaido said they were of Ainu descent. The majority have totally absorbed the Japanese way of life but many are working hard to record and maintain their ancient traditions before these are lost for ever. It is difficult for the Ainu to speak about their culture without describing their attitude to nature because the two are so closely entwined. Nature had provided everything that the people needed. In Hokkaido they hunted the brown bears and deer of the mountains and the foxes, rabbits and squirrels of the lowlands. They caught salmon from the rivers, and seals and sea-lions off the coast. Woman gathered nuts, fruit and vegetables to eat and bark to make clothes. The men built boats and frames for their homes from mature woodland trees and thatched them with reed from the marsh.

To the Ainu, natural phenomena, all living beings and objects, were gods or spirits known as *kamui*. The *kamui* lived in a world above the sky and some brought good things, some misfortune and others neither. The Ainu worshipped the things that were useful to them, believing that the gods had assumed their shape to bring them gifts. The gift of the bear god was his meat, his coat which kept them warm and his gall bladder which provided medicine. The call of the fishowl brought protection from calamity. The hierarchy of gods was determined by their relative usefulness. The Ainu understood the fundamental importance of the elements and of the sun and moon. Recognizing the essential role of natural habitats in providing food, they also worshipped the *kamui* of forests, lakes, mountains and rivers. The goddess of fire, who resided in the hearth, held a senior position. Useful plants such as vines and herbs had their own spirits and so did cooking bowls.

The brown bear god was one of the most highly respected since, as Lord of the mountains, he had power over the other creatures. If the bear god was well pleased he sent salmon down the rivers and deer down the mountains. When he visited the Ainu home, therefore, he had to be entertained so that he would return to the god world with good memories of the village and recommend it to others. First the bear had to be enticed into the home. In the ancient Ainu tale that follows (adapted from *The Romance of The Bear God* by Shigeru Kayano) the bear god is curious but does not enter the house completely of his own accord:

A bear with wanderlust comes down from the mountains. He is met by the beautiful goddess of pine resin and the goddess of the aconite. They give him an invitation from the goddess of fire to join her in the senior village house. The bear god is reluctant but, as he struggles against their persistence, the pine resin from one goddess becomes stuck to his body and he is overcome by the sweet smell from the other. He wakes up in a house and realizes that his gift of meat has already been taken, his skin flayed and his head cut off. But he, the bear god, sits between the ears of his old head. He is offered millet liquor, dumplings and dried fish. He is given gifts for his parents in the god world and is told exciting stories which are left unfinished so that he is eager to return. Eventually an arrow is shot into the eastern sky and he follows it back to the god world.

Previous page: Weeding the rice paddies in Miyazaki prefecture, Kyushu. Rice cultivation had a profound effect on the people's attitude to nature as they gradually changed from a hunter-gatherer to an agrarian lifestyle.

*An Ainu warrior in traditional costume prepares to dance the steps of the bow dance. The symbolic arrow which leads the **kamui** or spirit back to the god world is always fired towards the east.*

The story reflects the traditional methods the Ainu used to hunt bears: arrowheads poisoned with aconite were smeared with pine resin to make them stick.

Each winter, before the bear hunting season could begin, the Ainu celebrated the *Iomante*, the bear festival in which they returned a young bear to the god world. The bear was raised from a tiny cub with the children of the village. In olden days it was said that the cub suckled from a woman's breast.

In one Ainu village I was shown a film of a bear festival that had taken place in 1977, one of the last at which a bear was actually killed. (Japanese law now prohibits the sacrifice of bears at such festivals.) The villagers first collected birch, willow and vine branches from the forest, choosing a forked branch on which to rest the bear's head, and therefore, his spirit. Short branches of wood were then whittled away with a knife until curly streamers hung like the ribbons from a maypole to create the *inau*, the traditional decorative offering to the *kamui*. The young bear, having grown large and unruly, had been placed in a wooden cage. During the preparations many of the villagers stopped to talk to him and feed him titbits. On the eve of the festival they danced in their traditional costumes, stamping and clapping around the bear's cage to alert the gods. They then tied the young bear with ropes and dragged him from his cage.

The terrified bear snarled and tried to claw them. First the boys, then the warriors shot blunt arrows at him. The bear fought and foamed at the mouth until he became exhausted. Then the chief shot him in the heart with an arrow. (Traditionally the bear's neck was subsequently crushed between two heavy logs.) Great rejoicing and games such as tug-of-war ensued. The bear was then skinned and its meat prepared. Its head was placed on a mat at the centre of the table and it was offered *sake* to drink. The villagers drank a toast to the bear and began to feast. Then, following the tradition that the bear god should be entertained, they sang and danced merrily around the table. The bear's head was skinned and its brain removed. Bandaged with a patterned cloth and dressed with the wooden *inau*, it was placed on the fork of the branch. The branch was wrapped in a kimono and the bear placed outside in the centre of an altar flanked by animal skulls. At dawn his forehead was anointed and he was turned to face the east. An arrow was shot to lead his spirit back to the god world. The next day snow covered the bear. The kimono was removed and jays flocked in to peck at the remaining flesh on the skull.

After the Meiji restoration of 1868, and in increasing numbers since the Second World War, the Japanese flocked to Hokkaido which offered exciting opportunities to pioneers and land specu-lators tired of the claustrophobia of Honshu. Today, Hokkaido is thriving. Commercial fisheries and paper mills are huge concerns and industrial cities such as Sapporo and Kushiro are still expanding. The island has become the grain belt and dairy capital of Japan, producing around three-quarters of its potatoes, a third of its wheat, a quarter of its timber and almost half its milk. Huge areas of forest were cleared to make way for agriculture and many of the freshwater fish were poisoned by the run-off of agricultural pesticides into the rivers. The fishowl, (*Ketupa blakistoni*) was hit hard by the increasing human popu-lation and the change from hunter gathering to intensive farming.

In Ainu folklore the fishowl was the *kamui* and protector of the village. It was probably granted this role because it shared the same habitat as the Ainu – rivers full of fish which meander through forests providing shelter and nesting trees. Many Ainu villages were within the territory of a fishowl pair and the Ainu would have heard their comforting duet through the night.

During one visit to Hokkaido, I was given a rare treat and taken to see a fishowl family. I waded through the deep snow blanketing the woods at that magic hour before night falls, following the tracks of our guide, Sumio Yamamoto, whose concern is to protect and study the fishowl about which so little

Blakiston's fishowl with its young. One of the largest and rarest owls in the world, fishowls, like eagle owls, have distinctive ear tufts which ruffle in the breeze.

Fishowls wrestling over a fish on the frozen river. Throughout the year they supplement their fish diet with small mammals and birds and in early summer they take frogs.

is known. Fox tracks were visible in the snow and a hare loped off into the dark trees. We huddled silently waiting. The river was locked in ice and the only sound was the creaking as the ice dropped and resettled with the ebbing tide. We heard a call, surprisingly low and deep, 'oo hu'. The responding 'oo' echoed on a lower note, so close that it was as if one of us had replied. But it was the female completing the duet from her favourite tree. The dueting helps naturalists identify fishowl territory but when the female is without a partner she uses the male part of the duet, so the sexes can only be distinguished if the duet is completed. We could see the female clearly and I was amazed by her size, Blakiston's fishowl is one of the largest owls in the world – 71 cm tall and 4 kg in weight. The male flew behind us to land in a tall conifer. The young one, now six months old and almost as large as its parents, landed on our right. We were surrounded by three dark pear shapes high in the trees. Yamamoto shone a torch so that we could see the owls looking down. Transfixed by the bright yellow eyes, I had the uncanny feeling of being alone with the owl in the forest.

During the winter months fresh fish is placed on a bird table to supplement this pair's diet. The female flew in first and

27

gripped the fish with one clawed foot. The youngster followed and flew off with his prize. The male watched and waited. The creaking of the river suddenly became louder and more persistent. Perhaps a fox was interested in the fish. We went to investigate. The young owl was playing with a piece of wood on the frozen river. He tossed it up, lunged, then tossed again. He turned to look at us from three metres or so away and again I was gripped by those incredible eyes. Ignoring us, he tiptoed over to the wood. Lifting his shaggy feet high into the air and placing them delicately on the ice, bobbing as he went, he looked as if he were performing a comic dance. Then, as if to remind us he was an owl, he lifted his wings and flew majestically upwards,

past the hawfrost- and snow-laden branches, to perch high above us.

The fishowl only occurs north of Blakiston's Line. Naturalists estimate that there are between fifty and eighty fishowls left in Hokkaido with probably fewer than twenty pairs actually breeding and perhaps the same number again in the nearby Russian islands. For a large owl, which at best will produce one chick every two years, the situation is extremely grave. Today the bird is strictly protected but despite this it is still losing precious habitat: many rivers have been straightened and their sides concreted to control their flow, and natural woodland is still being replaced by forestry. In addition its breeding success is poor. Pesticides ingested from contaminated fish may explain why the eggs are sometimes infertile. Naturalists have pointed out that more could be done to protect the fishowl. Their experiments have shown that fishowls will breed successfully in artificial nestboxes placed in areas where there are no nesting holes and that the owls will also learn to take fish placed regularly in safe sites without abandoning their own hunting patterns. The Environment Agency is now funding some of this work. Many of the bird's traditional haunts are owned by the Forestry Agency, so the government is well placed to protect its habitat. Fish farms, which have been established on many rivers, could also be turned to the fishowls' advantage. A regular supply of fish would support the young, in particular, through their first winter.

Fishowls have long disappeared from most Ainu villages and lone owls call in vain as they search for a mate to complete the duet. The plight of the fishowl is mirrored by the plight of the Ainu. The Ainu had no written language and their history was passed down by reciting dramatic epics known as *yukar*. These are still performed today and in one the fishowl god sings the following verses:

> *I came down along the river stream*
> *Passing over the villages where people lived,*
> *I look down there.*
> *The poor in the past have become rich*
> *Whilst the rich in the past seem to be poorer.*

which tells the story of the modern-day disaster that has hit the Ainu. When the Japanese arrived they took ownership of the land, preventing the Ainu from hunting, fishing and tree-felling. They insisted that the Ainu learned Japanese at school and took Japanese names, and promoted Japanese customs. Unable to hunt, the Ainu were encouraged to farm. Yet the

Hokkaido is a land of high mountains thick forests and wide-flowing rivers, many of which have now been straightened and lined with concrete, rendering them uninhabitable for wildlife (see page 189).

Reciting the fishowl yukar, *the dramatic epic which tells how the fishowl was the first god to come down from the god world.*

Facing page: Carvings of brown bears, fishowls, foxes and all the wildlife symbols in Ainu culture are on sale at the 'Ainu village' near Lake Akan. Tiny marimo balls are sold in jars.

Japanese themselves shot thousands of deer and hundreds of brown bears, besides chopping down forests and exporting both hides and timber to the mainland.

When the Ainu discovered that my subject was Japan's wildlife and the people's attitude towards it they explained how, as hunters and fishermen, they had always lived in harmony with the land. They took only their daily requirement of salmon, waiting until the fish had spawned (when they would die anyway) before taking enough to smoke for the winter. They were taught by their parents not to throw waste into the rivers. They felled mature trees as they needed them and took bark from a small section of the tree, so that it would grow back. Before they felled, they asked the tree god's permission. The relationship between the gods and the Ainu was practical. A bear that would not be caught, or which killed children, was a bad god as was a tree which would not burn or was rotten. Bad gods were punished.

Today the large brown bear (*Ursus arctos*) still lives in the mountains of Hokkaido and is hunted not as a god but as a pest. Related to the grizzlies of North America, it has a ferocious reputation and can be shot both in self-defence and during the hunting season because of the damage it is said to do to forestry and agriculture. At places like a bear zoo near Lake Toya perhaps a hundred bears are crowded into a few concrete cages; safely behind bars they have become a tourist attraction.

In the past when the Ainu sacrificed a fishowl or celebrated the bear festival, they were doing the gods a favour by releasing them from the human world and sending them back to the god

Female brown bear with cubs. Few people would dare go this close to wild brown bears but Mamoru Odajima has spent years studying and photographing wild brown bears in Daisetsuzan National Park in central Hokkaido.

world. Thus the festival was a time of great rejoicing and celebration in which the bear god himself participated. The practice was a kind of spiritual game management – by returning what they had to the god world the people would receive manifold. This was the Ainu way of looking after the wildlife resources they needed. And from the point of view of conservation it was surely better than farming which, by its very existence, displaces nature.

Ainu beliefs and customs were practised in Hokkaido until the mid twentieth century when Japanese culture began to dominate. Yet ironically the remnants of their unique culture is one of the main sources of Ainu livelihood today. 'Ainu villages' are found in various parts of Hokkaido. Families run souvenir shops which sell carved wooden toys of bears, deer, foxes and fishowls. Ainu costumes can be rented for hire and photography. Tourists pay to watch *yukars* and dances in village halls, accompanied by the banging of drums and the wailing of the Jew's harp or of women. Festivals lasting two or three days are celebrated even though the animals that go through the ritual are no longer killed. Ainu from some villages dance and celebrate

solely for their own enjoyment. They believe that the sacred festivals should not be performed for tourists because they are insults to the gods.

The importance of festivals to the economy of some villages is illustrated by the story of the marimo. The marimo is a unique species of alga from Lake Akan which is rolled into tiny green balls by the current. The marimo grows to 10 cm in diameter and, as the inner filaments die, air pockets are formed and the balls float. The marimo was not traditionally worshipped by the Ainu because it was useless to them, often getting tangled in their fishing nets. After the Second World War, however, the marimo attracted the attention of scientists and its uniqueness encouraged tourists to take it home as souvenirs. One year a hydro-electric plant caused the level of Lake Akan to drop and the Ainu schoolchildren who liked to play with the balls found thousands stranded on the shore. They threw them back into the lake and a movement was formed to save the marimo. The Ainu now sell cultivated marimo in their shops.

Each year in a three-day festival they celebrate the rescue of the marimo. At the highpoint of the festival the Ainu proceed to the shores of the lake. They fire a symbolic arrow, then place the

On the shores of Lake Akan the Ainu celebrate the protection of the marimo. In the centre of the altar are the marimo and at the back are inau, *the sacred offerings to the* kamui *made by whittling short branches.*

marimo on the altar and offer sake and fruits to the marimo god. The village leaders row a boat across the lake and return the marimo to the water. I was told that this festival was simply a commercial venture with no links with past tradition. When I put this to one of the leaders in Akan village, he replied: 'In the past the marimo had no use but now it is useful. So it is right that we should return it to the gods and hold a festival in its honour.' Another explained: 'Our tradition was to live at one with the nature *kamui* and the marimo festival stands for the protection of our nature.'

                    *   *   *

All Japanese people inherit a strong reverence for nature. Shinto with its passion for natural beauty and Buddhism, which reveres all forms of life, are often presented as nature-loving religions. Signs of Shinto and Buddhism can be seen all over Japan. On rocks out to sea, on mountain summits and down in the valleys, the vermilion *torii*, Shinto gates or arches, stand out against the colours of nature. In the rice paddies and woods offerings of fruit and flowers are still placed before little wooden box shrines. In the cities a steady stream of businessmen pay homage to the tiny fox shrines, tucked between giant skyscrapers. The fox guards the shrine of the rice god but when business took over as the mainstay of many Japanese, they adopted the rice deity for themselves. Today in Japan there are over 80,000 temples and 100,000 shrines which regularly conduct ancient festivals and rituals. In speaking of their harmony with nature the Japanese contrast this with the western, Judaeo-Christian view, in which man, above and apart from nature, seeks to exploit and control it. Yet even the understanding of nature is based on different concepts. In Japan man, wildlife, the elements, the trees, the wooden buildings, the natural and even the artificial merged to create the physical world. Until Japan opened her doors in 1868 there was no direct translation of the western interpretation of 'nature'. It was not needed because nature was so much part of the people.

Shinto developed from a primitive form of animism. The Japanese story of creation is told through the deeds of the Shinto gods. In the beginning was the ocean. Two divine lovers plunged a spear into the waters and, as it rose, the drops fell and coagulated to become the islands of Japan. The divine lovers produced children known as *kami*. One of these, the sun goddess; Amaterasu o mi kami, was chosen to rule over the land. Japan's rulers were said to descend directly from her and were also *kami*. But the word *kami* is difficult to translate because in

Wooden **torii** *at the top of a ski slope in the Shiga Heights. Shinto* **torii** *or gates separate the spiritual world of the* **kami** *from the secular or ordinary. The character for* **torii** *is built from the words for bird and home.*

Facing page: The nature **kami** *were numinous, born of beauty and existing solely because they evoked feelings of fascination and awe.*

Shinto so many things, from the lowliest of men to the tallest of trees, had the qualities which made them *kami*. In the *kami* world there was no distinction between the living and non-living, animate and inanimate. A *kami* was something that evoked a feeling of beauty and awe. A gnarled and bent pine tree, a fox or a wolf, an appealingly placed stone, a waterfall or pool could all be *kami*, as could a natural arch or a twisted rock out at sea. Fujisan was a *kami*, as were many gorges and rivers, the wind and the rain. The belief that something was a *kami* was both spontaneous and passionate, evoked perhaps by a trick of the light and born of beauty.

The worship of *kami*, born of a fascination with their beauty rather than of fear, distinguishes Shinto from many other early religions. In many of these the most important gods were powerful and greatly feared, worshipped in order to placate them and to prevent the damage their anger could wreak. In Shinto there was no all-powerful evil spirit but there were many naughty ones. In the creation story the thunder *kami* behaved badly, destroying the paths that ran between the rice fields and insulting the sun goddess. There is no suggestion, however,

that his behaviour was caused by anger nor was anything done to appease him. Instead the thunder *kami* was punished by the other heavenly *kami* and banished to the land of darkness.

Shinto is essentially optimistic: daily activities such as eating, sex and family life are to be enjoyed. It is a religion of the living, concerned with this life rather than other worlds such as nirvana or heaven. Theologians have explained the basic optimism behind Shinto by relating it to the environment at the time the young religion was fostered. Many religions were born of the need for extra strength to face a hostile environment: the desert, the wilderness, the cold, or the long, dark nights of the north. To some of the tribes who founded early Japan it must have seemed like a promised land – fertile, rich and bountiful – compared to the dry regions of Korea or the inhospitable plains of northern China from whence they may have come. In Japan there was plenty to give praise for as some of the names given to the land in mythology indicate: 'the land of luxuriant reed plains' and 'the land of fresh rice ears of a thousand autumns'. Similarly the names of gods are full of promise: 'Princess Blossoming Like the Flowers of the Trees' and 'Her Augustness Myriad Looms Luxuriant Dragonfly Island.'

Shinto made a clear distinction between purity, fertility and growth, as opposed to the dead, the dirty, the polluted and the sick. Before the people could communicate with the *kami*, they had to remove impurities, by cleansing themselves. Every Japanese understands the significance in a drama when unfaithful men or women subject themselves to the biting shards of a waterfall.

As Shinto became more sophisticated, ropes of plaited rice straw adorned with hanging pieces of bleached mulberry bark were tied around the special tree or stone to define its *kami* nature. Later still wooden shrines were built to venerate the *kami*. Some large Shinto shrines enthrone particular gods, such as the Ise shrine in Nara prefecture, the seat of Amaterasu. Others, like the Toshogu at Nikko, enshrine emperors or shoguns, and yet others devote themselves solely to natural beauty, such as the Kumano Nachi grand shrine in Wakayama prefecture which reveres the Nachi waterfalls.

Animals became either gods or messengers of the gods of various Shinto cults. Mountain summits were holy places where, finding isolation and beauty, people could become purified. On remote mountain ranges such as Mitsumine, west of Tokyo, the howling wolves were divine messengers. In Kyoto, monkeys became the disciples of the mountain shrines (see Chapter 2). In Nara, the ancient capital, a deer carried the prince

Strips of white paper representing purity were used to define the dwelling place of a **kami**. *Although origami is generally thought to have been introduced from China, some scholars have related its popularity to the Shinto practice of folding paper into interesting shapes.*

on his back to the Kasuga shrine. In the lowlands, the fox found plenty of food in the ditches and scrub that skirted the rice paddies and became the messenger of the rice *kami*, Inari.

One of the principal fox shrines is Fushimi Inari in Kyoto where two large fox statues guard the main entrance. The Inari fox usually has a bushy tail, which symbolizes many fruitful ears of rice, and it carries a jewel in its mouth which represents the spirit of the deity. A second fox carries a key, the key to the wealth of the rice granary. The foxes are offered delicacies such as fried bean curd, which is why many wear bibs. I visited Fushimi Inari at dusk when the lanterns were lit and the vermilion buildings seemed to glow with magic like the eyes of the fox. The path through the woods which now surround Fushimi Inari is lined with miniature fox shrines and fox statues in many guises donated by the faithful. Today, because of the association of the shrines with business and prosperity there are over 30,000 active shrines related to Fushimi Inari alone.

The animal messengers are still very much in evidence. At Hiyoshi shrine in Kyoto, the sacred monkeys are kept in a cage. Deer protected by the Kasuga shrine still roam the streets of Nara. At many shrines visitors buy *ema*, wooden pictures of the

Facing page: Miniature fox statues in the grounds of Fushimi Inari in Kyoto. When the farmers left the rice paddies to become businessmen they kept the fox, messenger of the rice **kami,** *as the key to prosperity.*

messenger of the shrine, upon which they write wishes.

For many of the people I spoke to the most significant contribution of Shinto was its concept of the oneness of man with nature. Man, alongside the plants and animals, nestles in the lap of the physical world and some take this to imply that they are on the same plane or even equal. Thus Japanese people say it is easy for them to sympathize with wild animals. This theme, suggested by the poem at the beginning of this chapter, recurred in many conversations.

Another gift of Shinto which remains deeply embedded in the Japanese consciousness is a love of the seasons. The seasonal cycle reinforced the belief that nature would always replenish itself and provide what was needed. When the Japanese began to plant rice they had to pay meticulous attention to the signals which heralded a change of weather. Hundreds of local seasonal events, which developed from Shintoist agricultural rites, are still celebrated throughout Japan. In Nara prefecture, the summer lily festival has been observed since the days when the purity of the lily was believed to drive away pestilence. In the north children sing bird-chasing songs at New Year to keep birds off the young rice seedlings

The passing of the year is still pinpointed by the blossoming of flowers and other seasonal changes. In May, the azaleas flower and in June the irises bloom; as they fade the rains arrive. Late summer is the time for firefly watching at dusk (a practice curtailed when many firefly sites were destroyed by pesticides and the straightening of rivers). In August the hot, sticky weather brings out the crickets, many of which are kept as singing pets. The September typhoons clear the air and *susuki*, one of the seven grasses of autumn, flowers as thousands

Fox ema *at Fushimi Inari in Kyoto. The custom of writing wishes on the back of wooden pictures developed from the tradition of donating horses to shrines. People who could not afford real horses sketched them on pieces of wood.*

Flowering susuki, *one of the seven grasses symbolic of autumn. An arrangement of the seven grasses is often placed with the sweet white dumplings as offerings to the moon during September and October.*

of people begin 'autumn colour-viewing'. The geese migrate south ahead of the snow, hailing shorter winter days and clear skies. In February plum blossom signals that warmer weather is on its way.

The customs of the Japanese developed in response to the changes in their nature *kami*. The blossoming of the cherry trees in April on the main island of Honshu still heralds the beginning of the new school term, the movement of employees to new postings and the annual fight for wage increases. The 'cherry blossom-viewing' picnic is the most famous seasonal event when friends, families and colleagues gather together to drink and make merry under the trees. Nature being fickle, it is impossible to know exactly when the blossom will be at its best. News bulletins follow its progress as it moves in a tide up country, beginning in Okinawa as early as February and flowering in Hokkaido as late as June. The timing is critical because the full blooms fall quickly, harsh wind or rain destroying them overnight. Near a weekend when the trees are a delicate pink, employees are sent to famous 'cherry blossom-viewing' sites such as the Peace Park in Hiroshima to stake out a picnic area with ribbons and mats. They snooze night and day waiting for the revellers. Some arrive for lunch complete with music systems and microphones but it is at night that the singing, dancing and drinking reaches its climax and the spontaneous and passionate, more Shinto side of the Japanese character is released.

This reverence for the changing seasons has led people to describe the Japanese as continuing to live in harmony with nature. But what kind of influence has Shinto actually had on the country's attitude to wildlife and natural habitats? The

'Cherry blossom-viewing' picnickers at Hiroshima Peace Park. The arrival of the cherry blossom has been celebrated since an imperial decree in the eighth century. Everyone is welcome to join in the revelry and take part in the popular custom of **Karaoke** *– handing the microphone round for an impromptu song.*

belief that animals were sacred messengers and the empathy people have with wild animals has not protected some of them from persecution. The wolves, guardians of Mount Mitsumine, were shot to extinction soon after the beginning of the Meiji era. To the westerner there appears to be a dichotomous attitude to a number of animals such as deer, monkeys and foxes. The Japanese tend to describe the fox as a cunning trickster, rather than a benevolent messenger of the rice *kami*. The fox was believed to have the power of possession; he could enter into a person making them do bad things they would not normally do and causing all sorts of trouble. Many stories describe the wickedness of the fox, often hand in hand with that of the badger-like racoon dog. Certain families were believed to 'own' foxes who performed malicious deeds on their behalf and in a few cities like Matsue in southwest Honshu this superstition still affects social relationships between some families.

The wild fox is generally unpopular, regarded as a pest and heavily persecuted, particularly in Hokkaido where foxes are believed to carry diseases harmful to humans. As one person explained patiently, for many Japanese there is no inherent contradiction in their attitude to the fox. The Shinto fox may be shaped like a fox but he is actually the messenger or spirit of the rice *kami*. The malicious fox spirit bears the name of fox but appears in so many guises that he rarely looks like a fox. Neither has any relation in the minds of most Japanese to the real fox. Yet a natural history film made in 1978 showing the life of a family of foxes from the foxes' point of view is said to be largely responsible for improving the animal's image. Wildlife films and books, which we would describe as anthropomorphic, are common in modern Japan and the writers say that it comes naturally to them to put themselves in the animals' position. In the past there was surely a link between the symbol and the wild animal and there may be so increasingly in the future. Yet in 1984 the official number of foxes shot or captured in Japan was still over 15,000.

Shinto has played a significant role in protecting certain habitats simply by protecting the land which is under the jurisdiction of shrines. Over the centuries virtually every scrap of lowland Japan has been utilized but the wild beauty within some shrine precincts has remained sacred and untouched. The best remnants of lowland broad-leaved evergreen forest are found around Shinto shrines such as Ise, Nikko and Kasuga. In the courtyards tall cedars over a thousand years old stand girdled by plaited straw ropes. Behind them a mosaic of camellias, azaleas and hundreds of different shrubs and trees stretches into the hills, a memorial to the infinite variety of the lost forests.

Rare flowers, birds and insects continue to thrive in these shrine forests, part of which, as at Ise, are so sacred that the public is not allowed to walk through them. Many small mammals, such as the giant flying squirrel (*Petaurista leucogenys*), have benefited. A creature of mature lowland forests, it eats buds, blossoms, insects and even persimmons when they are in season and nests in the natural holes of ancient trees. It moves around by racing to the top of a tall tree and launching itself across to another, using flaps of skin between its fore and hind legs as a parachute. The squirrel is shy, nocturnal and sensitive to disturbance. When the native forests were felled the giant flying squirrels lost their habitat and today the best place to see them is near an ancient shrine. In a hilly area a few hours west of Tokyo four small ancient shrines provide a home for a family of giant flying squirrels which nest in the eaves.

It might be expected that Shinto would provide an ideal basis for protecting many wild habitats. Oneness with nature is often used to imply harmony or non-interference with nature. Yet it could be argued that with the increasing pressure to take land

While most of Japan's lowland forest was displaced by agriculture, the shrine forests (protected by the presence of **kami**) *became wildlife sanctuaries.*

for agriculture or homes, no religion could stand up to habitat destruction. The answer to the apparent contradiction in Japanese attitudes may run deeper – Shinto itself may be the root cause of what seems, even today, to be a generally passive attitude towards the natural world. At worst equal status with a living thing can bring a desire to fight and control it and even if oneness does not lead to domination, it might lead to an ambivalent position, a sense that a being of the same status should be able to take care of itself. The Japanese have survived the disasters of earthquake, volcano, wind and flood. Like the parable of the bamboo which bends with the typhoon but straightens after the wind has passed, why should nature not now survive the changes caused by man?

*   *   *

Buddhism originated in India, then spread to China and Korea and under royal patronage gained its first strong foothold in Japan in the sixth century. The imperial family embraced Buddhism because of its links with the superior and sophisticated government and culture of the great Chinese empire. Japanese envoys were sent to China to learn about this great civilization and Chinese and Korean immigrants came to Japan as teachers. The Japanese had no written language and they began to copy and adapt the Chinese characters using Buddhist sutras as their teaching tools. By the eighth century, when Nara was established as the capital, Buddhism and central government control were firmly entwined. But there was a clear division between the court and the countryside, where the old Shinto magic prevailed.

Buddhism, however, had other ways of extending its influence. Buddhist temples were affiliated to the state and the monks became powerful land owners. People were registered at temples and paid taxes through them in the form of rice and other crops. The philosophical side of Buddhism was out of the reach of ordinary people but they were drawn to the large smiling Buddhas, the images that protected them against calamities, and the pomp and gold of Buddhism as compared with the simplicity of Shinto. The problem of antagonizing the native Shinto deities was solved by incorporating them into Buddhist belief, each Buddha becoming a manifestation of a Shinto deity; thus Amaterasu, the sun goddess, was the incarnation of the all-powerful solar Buddha, Dainichi. Gradually many people came to see the two religions as complementary.

The basic doctrine of early Indian Buddhism is that there is suffering throughout life, caused by human desire and prolonged

A monk from the Buddhist Tendai sect at Son-sho-in in Kyoto. Tendai is more concerned than most sects of Buddhism with ritual and symbolism and was introduced to Japan from Mount Hiei, home of the sacred monkey messengers (see page 55).

by an endless cycle of reincarnation. The final stage of release, nirvana, is extremely difficult to attain although the Buddha reached it. In Japan Buddhism, already transformed by the Chinese, became a more optimistic religion. Release or enlightenment could be achieved without having to fast or meditate for months in isolation and Buddhahood became a possibility for every living being. Deer, snails and even flies could be reborn up the scale until they reached enlightenment and nirvana. If a man killed a deer he might move down the scale and become a deer in his next reincarnation; the taking of any life was shameful.

From the Nara period onwards Buddhism encouraged the eating of fish and vegetarian food as opposed to red meat and over the years this alone must have saved thousands of wild animals. Its influence did not stop ruling aristocrats like the shoguns from protecting certain areas where they could hunt wild game. Neither could it change the fact that birds which trampled seedlings and insects and deer which nibbled crops were the farmers' enemies. Yet strong traces of the special Buddhist reverence for life remain. Animal funerals are still held in some institutions such as the Kyoto Primate Research Centre

This Buddhist pagoda stands in the forest above the Itsukushima shrine at Miyajima. Perhaps because of the ancient Shinto reverence for the nature kami, *in Japan every living being as well as trees and even mountains had the potential to become a Buddha.*

to pray for the souls of monkeys killed in research. Religious merit could be gained by releasing trapped and injured animals. Today, on 15 September each year, a Buddhist-influenced ceremony known as Hōjōe is held at the Shinto Iwashimizu Hachiman shrine in Kyoto when priests release caged budgerigars and parakeets and families drop an assortment of fish into a pond. In days gone by people scoured the countryside to catch animals to release; thousands of songbirds died before reaching the festival. At bridges passers-by were encouraged to buy pond turtles to release which the enterprising sellers caught for resale downstream.

Buddhism was able to detach itself from nature and yet take deep inspiration from it. The lotus, for example, one of the most famous Buddhist symbols, is used to express the infinite depths of man's wisdom. It is a flower of pure and simple beauty, standing still and apart from the muddy waters from which it feeds and from which it rose. Man, if he stilled his thoughts of desire, could like the lotus clear his mind of the muddy waters of the world.

Zen is the Buddhist sect especially renowned for its strong accord with nature. Introduced from China in the twelfth century, it differed from other Buddhist philosophies in a number of important ways. It did not have the numerous idols of mainstream Buddhism and enlightenment was gained through self-examination rather than by reading scriptures or chanting incantations. Observing an event in nature, or creating a clever riddle of words such as the renowned 'Listen to the sound of one hand clapping' might jolt one into enlightenment. Zen was said to appeal to the Japanese because its open embrace of the unity of man with nature found sympathy with their Shinto ideals and its practice of gentle contemplation suited their aesthetic sensibilities. The concept of *wabi*, the richness and therefore desirability of poverty, comes from Zen.

The self-awakening attained through Zen was individual and the early Zen monks climbed into the mountains to lose the physical trappings of civilization and free their minds from the disturbance of others. The natural world was ideal for contemplation, inspiration, poverty, self-denial and the triumph of the natural over the artificial. The highest form of spiritual attainment was said to be gained through the contemplation of the wonders of nature. And the Zen monks possibly accorded nature the deepest spiritual contemplation it has had in the history of mankind. Yet, nature was not contemplated for its own sake but to release knowledge of man's infinite depths. Enlightened people have written that the trees and flowers glow and sing; Buddha's voice can be heard in the flow of the stream, the mountains are his body and the shining stars his eyes.

While Zen encouraged originality and even eccentricity, Confucianism, which was absorbed from China together with

A Zen-inspired moss garden, iridescent green against bare trees, illustrates the concept of the **wabi** *or joy of simplicity.*

Buddhism, continued to encourage the belief that the group was more important than the individual. Confucianism brought order, philosophy and rationalization to temper the instinctive passion of Shinto. I quickly became aware in my visits to the national parks that 'nature-viewing' was for many Japanese a group activity.

Today many of the holy mountains have become popular tourist attractions. Mount Nantai, which towers over Lake Chuzenji in Nikko National Park, was once a remote Shinto *kami*. In the eighth century, Shodo, a Buddhist monk, came to

Mount Nantai in Nikko National Park. The best place to see Shodo's vision is from the Senjogahara marshes.

Nantai. Looking up he saw clouds rising from its peak and knew that he had found a holy place. It took him fourteen years to reach the summit. He named the mountain 'the pure land' and carved a path up it for others to follow. At that time Nikko was badly affected by drought and on the summit of Nantai Shodo prayed for rain. Legend has it that it fell in a vast torrent and the lake overflowed creating the sacred Kegon falls. At the foot of Nantai stands a Shinto shrine and close by there is a Buddhist temple.

Today a zigzag road, famed for 'autumn colour-viewing', takes coachloads of 'pilgrims' through Nikko. The pressure is on to pack as many sights in as possible and few have time to climb the steps of the famous Toshogu shrine to the quiet solitude of the shogun's tomb watched over by the symbolic crane and turtle. Above, away from the crowds, the graceful golden roofs of the shrine merge with the tall evergreen trees in a brief glimpse of the ancient harmony. The tour does allow time for a group photograph and a lake cruise to view the concreted slopes of Nantai. Travelling down to the Kegon falls by lift, the tourists reach a tiered viewing platform complete with souvenir shops. Postcards of falling torrents set against brilliant autumn colours are on sale. But concrete crosshatching covers the flanks of the gorge leaving just enough space for a narrow portrait-format photograph of the pristine waterfall. When the last tourist has gone the falls are turned off.

In Japan Buddhism and Shinto sometimes found common ground in their attitude to the natural world. For instance the Buddhist attitude that life is transient was sympathetic to the Shinto tenet of continual cleansing and renewal. This was brought home to me one rainy evening in Tokyo when Dr Stuart Picken, an authority on the religions of Japan, likened fallen cherry blossoms to the ephemerality of life in Buddhism and their being carried away by a river to the Shinto flow of purity, an image which we were to witness at the Hiroshima Peace Park. Perhaps in a similar way, the Buddhist belief that life is about suffering links to the Shinto promise that nature will always replenish itself and provide what is needed: a bird that has lost its first clutch will generally lay a second time; a path that is cleared of vegetation will be overgrown again the following year. In 1890 when the Japanese provided a word to describe the western meaning for nature they chose *shizen* meaning spontaneity or 'from itself, thus it is'. The belief that death and destruction are facts of life and that nature will always recover of her own accord may contribute to a generally passive and pragmatic attitude towards nature, fostering the

Toshogu shrine in Nikko: away from the crowds the roofs merge with the cedars offering a rare glimpse of ancient harmony. In neither Shinto nor Buddhism was there the belief that man had been given dominion over nature.

Facing page: *The sacred Kegon falls in Nikko which overflow from Lake Chuzenji. Today the waters of the lake are needed to generate hydro-electricity for the area's hotels and shops and when the tourists have left the falls are turned off.*

idea that nature will take care of herself.

Japanese writers and politicians continue to declare that they are in harmony with nature and that plants and animals are their brothers. They are indeed at 'one' with the natural world but at the same time they are at 'one' with the world as a whole, the mountains, the highways, the new cars and the robots. Just as the people have to share, nature is also expected to give ground. And if man is part of nature, then human actions, whether planting a forest or destroying a mountain, are also 'natural'.

The nature-revering practices of Shinto and Buddhism evolved in the days when nature was able to replenish itself in the yearly cycle of the seasons. More and more people are realizing that, against the linear and progressive onslaught of industrialization and consumerism, nature has little chance. The Japanese now have the power of volcanoes or gods to create new landscapes; they no longer have to live in harmony with nature. Like Christianity, neither Shinto, Buddhism nor the Ainu *kamui* provides the answer for the environmental problems the world faces today. Yet they do offer promise – a strong awareness of and reverence for the wonders of nature – without which there would be no such thing as conservation.

SEE NO EVIL

In the beginning was the macaque and then came the ancestors of the Japanese. Macaques probably arrived when Japan was attached to the Eurasian continent over a million years ago. At some stage in the isolation of Japan, a shaggy, short-tailed species, the Japanese macaque (*Macaca fuscata*) evolved. The adaptable monkey colonized most of the archipelago, from sub-tropical Yakushima, a small island south of Kyushu, to the deciduous forests of the northern tip of Honshu.

Today the macaque is essentially a mountain creature but,

Haniwa clay monkey, c. 400 AD. This female monkey is thought originally to have carried a baby and anthropologists have suggested that the figure is linked to a belief that monkeys had powers to promote fertility. (Courtesy of Tatsuo Nakazawa)

like the Japanese serow (*Capricornis crispus*) and Asiatic black bear (*Selenarctos thibetanus*), it once found its living in the rich lowland forests. Recovered bones show that macaques lived in the area which is now Tokyo. Rice cultivation displaced the lowland forests, driving the large mammals away from the plains and, later, from the hills. As the people settled down to cultivate the land, the monkeys were forced to live in the remote mountains. Conflict developed between them as the opportunist monkey troops added rice and vegetables to their diet, converging on the fields in large bands and disappearing quickly with hands and cheeks stuffed with food.

Bones discovered in Jōmon settlements indicate that the people ate monkeys. Monkey bones fashioned into earrings and pendants have also suggested to historians that a belief in the monkey's special powers dates back to the Jōmon period. Hunting and eating monkeys was generally outlawed when Buddhism became established in the seventh century but the practice continued in a few remote areas of the northern alps until it was officially banned in 1947. Ground and powdered monkey was favoured as a cure for women's ailments until modern times. Professor Hirose, whose studies of the wealth of monkey folklore reveal an ambivalent attitude to the monkey, has pointed out that through history the Japanese have never quite been sure whether the monkey is a good or an evil omen. In the Shinto story of the creation the grandson of the sun goddess comes down to found the earth to discover his way blocked by a frightening god 'whose back was more than seven fathoms', a light shines 'from his mouth and from his posteriors'. But the beast, often known as the 'monkey god', had only come to greet and guide the heavenly party. Shinto monkey-chasing festivals are still practised in some areas. In the Odaka shrine at Hanasaki the role of the monkey is played by a man from the same family each year. The villagers chase him round the shrine three times mimicking the countless times they have chased monkeys away from their crops. Interestingly the monkey always escapes and the ritual has become a kind of harvest festival, a way of ensuring that the crops will be blessed the following year.

Not surprisingly, few ancient folk tales favour the monkey. Described as mean and cunning, it is invariably regarded as an enemy. Yet, while conflict between man and monkey increased, belief in the divine powers of monkeys grew. On Mount Hiei, a sacred Shinto mountain northeast of the old capital, Kyoto, the macaques became messengers communicating between the Shinto priests and the *kami* or spirits of the mountains. One story tells how, when the people went to speak with the *kami*,

At Hiyoshi shrine on Mount Hiei in accordance with an old tradition a Shinto priest offers fruit to the **kami** *of the waterfall. In ancient times wild macaques (which still live in these forests) would have removed the fruit.*

wild monkeys appeared from the forest as if the *kami* had manifested itself in the monkey. Another describes how, when offerings of fruit and vegetables were placed before the *kami*, it was the wild monkeys who were sent to collect them.

Hiyoshi shrine on Mount Hiei is the headquarters of the Shinto sect that still worships the monkey as a divine messenger. High in the mountains and deep in the shady forest, Hiyoshi, with its peeling red paint, has the atmosphere of ancient mystery. Legend says that monkeys helped carry the timber for the buildings. Monkey figures guard Hiyoshi and decorate the small golden shrine reserved for festivals. Carved monkeys hold up the roofs of shrines of the same sect which can be found in various parts of the countryside.

Mount Hiei was an important early mixing ground for Shinto and Buddhism. Late in the eighth century a young priest, Saichō, brought up in the Shinto environment of Mount Hiei, became a Buddhist novice. After travelling to China to study with the esoteric Tendai Buddhist sect, he returned to introduce its teachings to Japan. Sympathetic to the Shinto beliefs of his childhood and believing that Shinto and Buddhism could live

Guardian monkey at Sekizan Zen-in temple in Kyoto whose job was to protect the imperial palace from bad influences which in the eighth century, when Kyoto was made the new capital, came from the northeast.

and join in harmony, he prayed to the Shinto *kami* of Hiei before building a temple in AD 788, known as Enryakuji, at the summit of the mountain. Hiyoshi, home of the divine monkeys, was later made the guardian shrine of Enryakuji.

When Emperor Kammu moved his court from Nara to Heian (Kyoto) in AD 794, the importance of the monkeys of Hiei increased. Although becoming a follower of Saichō, the emperor seems to have preferred the magic of Shinto to the philosophical aspect of early Tendai. The monkey was chosen to protect the imperial palace from bad spirits. A carved monkey holding a *gohei*, a Shinto purification wand, sits on the northeast corner of the palace wall facing Hiyoshi and Enryakuji, the direction from which evil influences were thought to come. And at various temples between Enryakuji and Kyoto there are carved monkeys to protect the imperial family. Popular theory attributes the choice of the monkey to the Japanese delight in play on words: both the (Chinese) characters for monkey 猿 and for 'to go away' or 'to remove' 去 are pronounced in Japanese as 'saru', and so in a pun the monkey came to symbolize the chasing away of evil. But perhaps the emperor was also influenced in his choice by the importance of the sacred monkeys on Hiei.

As monkeys featured so prominently in the beliefs of the Kyoto people, it is not surprising that the monks of the new

Buddhist doctrines chose macaques to help spread the word. About a century after Saichō's death, a monk named Ganzan came down from Enryakuji and established a temple in Kyoto, Son-sho-in. According to legend, he wrote the seven-stanza poem (translated at the beginning of this chapter), known as 'the seven-monkey poem', to convey the eclectic teachings of Tendai to a public who could not read. Some scholars have suggested, however, that the poem is more likely to have been written long after Ganzan's death in the Edo period by a monk who was trying to rekindle an interest in Tendai. Whatever its date, the poem has obvious links with the famous three wise monkeys who see, speak and hear no evil.

The monkey poem uses a play on words to convey its meaning. In the last verse, for example, the three negatives have become 'the three monkeys'. This time the monkey symbolizes the negative verb inflection 'zaru' or 'not' so that a monkey together with a verb becomes the negative of that verb. A monkey figure with its hands over its eyes makes the meaning doubly clear. So the three wise monkeys symbolize *zaru* in the combination, *Mizaru*, do not see evil, or 'see no evil', *Kikazaru*, 'hear no evil' and *Iwazaru*, 'speak no evil'.

The three wise monkeys. Profound yet lovable they have charmed people all over the world. But what special blend of ideas and circumstances inspired their origination?

Four wise monkeys at Son-sho-in in Kyoto. At some stage the original design must have been copied and replaced, but does the fourth monkey provide a vital clue or is it a more recent addition?

Most Japanese people associate the three wise monkeys with a play on words, yet at the same time, perhaps because they have heard so often that much of their culture is Chinese in origin, many believe that the three monkeys come from China. But the link between the pronunciation for monkey and for the negative does not exist in China.

In fact the origin of the three monkeys is shrouded in mystery; they have been claimed to originate in India, Cambodia and even Egypt and other parts of Africa as well as in China. According to one legend the original wise monkeys are housed at Ganzan's little-known Son-sho-in temple in Kyoto. I visited the temple, only to find four monkeys rather than three. The fourth, his hands in an ambivalent posture, perhaps depicts the final lines of the poem 'not thinking is by far the best'.

At Rozan-ji, another temple in Kyoto related by legend to Ganzan, two carved screens actually depict a total of seven monkeys, the number of stanzas in Ganzan's poem. One screen shows three monkeys sitting together, the second reveals the three wise monkeys but again with the addition of a fourth 'thinking' monkey. To trace a plausible story for the three wise monkeys, I had to find an explanation for the disappearance of the fourth.

Today the three wise monkeys are most closely associated with Koshin, a Taoist cult which came from China in the Heian period. According to Koshin belief, three worms inhabit the body, emerging every sixty days on Koshin eve to report evil doings to a heavenly god, hoping to shorten their host's life and so be free of the host's body. The way to outwit the dastardly worms is to stay awake on Koshin eve. This custom, first patronized by the aristocracy, was later taken up by the samurai or warrior class and around the fifteenth century it became a popular folk belief among rural villagers. Koshin eve was known as monkey night because, according to the ancient oriental dating system based on the cycle of five elements and twelve animals, it fell on the day that metal coincided with monkey.

Dr George Hlawatsch, an American academic living in Kyoto, believes that monkeys were first used as a Koshin symbol, then at a later stage, perhaps in the seventeenth century, the three wise monkeys were adopted as a cheerful antidote to the three evil worms. They might have been sculpted to help protect the people against the wicked worms or as a reminder to them to behave themselves.

Until recently Koshin remained a powerful force in the countryside. In Kunisaki peninsula, in Kyushu, I was shown some Koshin stones that were carved in the early eighteenth century; only in the last few years had the paths become overgrown with brambles and some stones still had fruits or flowers placed before them. Some carvings depicted a monkey and a cock; cock-crow was the signal that monkey night was over. Others had three or four dancing monkeys and many were illustrated with the three wise monkeys. In some villages monkey-night vigils are still respected. In one area of Tokyo's high-rise suburbs the Koshin stones were rescued and placed together, rather like tombstones, before the land was built on and a small group of believers still take turns to host Koshin night. They pray facing a scroll of the three-monkey image, then they relax, eat, drink and return home. The Koshin temple in Osaka hosts a festival each Koshin eve. At the one in Kyoto, known locally as the monkey temple, three large wise monkeys sit in front of a screen used rather like an altar. Hanging from it are strings of hand-made monkey dolls brought by those praying for the sick. Monkey dolls are thought to be particularly lucky in one's nineteenth year of life.

Three monkeys would match three worms better than four and Koshin may well have been responsible for spreading the

Koshin stone in Kunisaki peninsula, Kyushu. Shomen Kongo, one of the more fearsome of the Buddhist pantheon, was adopted by Koshin believers as a focus of worship, possibly (as with the wise monkeys) to protect the people from the three terrible worms.

three-monkey image throughout Japan. It may have been the monks of Mount Hiei who, looking for popular religions through which to spread their doctrines, suggested the initial link between the three monkeys and Koshin. If so, the popularity of the three monkeys could be linked to the divine monkey messengers of Mount Hiei.

In 1617 monks from Enryakuji on Hiei travelled north to Nikko to help set up the mausoleum and shrine known as Toshogu, in honour of one of the great shoguns, Tokugawa Ieyasu. Some 15,000 craftsmen, many from Kyoto, which was still the cultural and religious centre of Japan, helped to create the lavish complex of buildings. They brought with them the concept of the three monkeys. The three wise monkeys carved above the stable at Nikko are probably the most famous in the world. They are part of a panorama of eight reliefs, each depicting a scene from the life history of the monkey. Published interpretations of the scenes suggest Buddhist and Confucian over-

*Monkey dolls hanging from a screen at the Koshin temple in Kyoto. Monkey dolls were made by women of nineteen and were thought to ward off the bad luck associated with this **Yakudoshi** or unlucky year.*

One of a series of eight reliefs above the stable at the Toshogu shrine in Nikko. The monkeys represent stepping stones in the life of man. A monkey, no longer youthful, plans to take a gamble: he cannot swim but he is about to jump into the sea. His friend is advising him not to be so reckless.

tones of good behaviour. The monkey on the fourth relief, for example, gazes into the distance and is described as ambitious, thinking of his future social position and wealth. The eighth relief shows a newly born monkey, suggesting that the life cycle begins again after death.

The placing of the monkeys over the stable refers to a belief which originated in China. According to legend a monkey cured a Chinese emperor's horse, leading to the conviction that monkeys had the power to protect livestock from disease. As a result, monkey skulls were pinned inside stables (a custom practised until recently in the mountains north of Takayama).

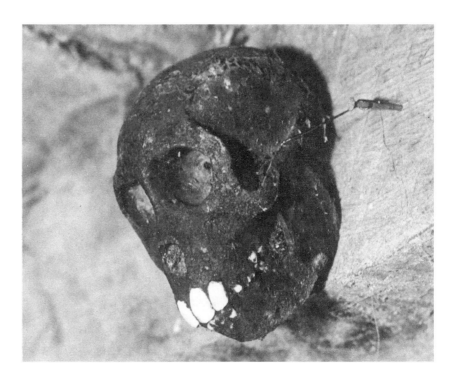

Monkey skulls were pinned to stable eaves in the northern alps in the belief that they would protect livestock from sickness.

Many Japanese mistakenly think that the trio at Nikko was the original carving of the three monkeys in Japan. While Koshin was responsible for spreading the three monkeys throughout Japan, since the Meiji restoration foreign visitors have flocked to Nikko and Dr Hlawatsch has traced references which suggest that it was from Nikko that the three wise monkeys spread (or returned) to the rest of the modern world.

With their diverse connotations, the three wise monkeys still charm people in many continents. It is easy to see why they were so popular in medieval Japan; they epitomized the personal restraint and prudence of the samurai and they struck a chord with the Confucian rules for good behaviour and filial piety. That the interpretation of the fourth monkey was flexible is suggested by the following verses which are attributed to the priest Muju (*c.* 1305):

> *My eyes cannot see*
> *My ears cannot hear*
> *I cannot make a sound*
> *The three monkeys are indeed*
> *Easy to maintain*
>
> *Not speaking and*
> *Not seeing, not hearing –*
> *Compared to these*
> *Not thinking is indeed*
> *Hard to maintain.*

A comic verse from the eighteenth century offers another interpretation:

> *Sleeplessly*
> *Sitting up late*
> *On Koshin eve*
> *Koshin includes 'do nothing'*
> *As a fourth monkey*

The popularity of the three-monkey motif, from wherever it originally derived, appears to have been more widespread in Japan, during the five hundred years before her shores were re-opened to outsiders in 1868, than anywhere else.

*　　　*　　　*

Today wild monkeys still live in Nikko, now a national park, and in the forests of Mount Hiei. The Japanese macaque is a social animal living in troops numbering from fifteen to two hundred or more. The social structure is highly organized; each monkey knows his or her own position in relation to the other

Most infant Japanese macaques are born during the night. For the first five or six months when the troop moves the baby clings to its mother's front, then graduates to riding on her back. Even after a year, at any sign of danger it returns immediately to its mother's back.

members of the troop and recognizes outsiders. At the core a dominant male leads a hierarchy of males and related females. Little overt aggression is needed to maintain this but who grooms whom, who displaces whom from the choicest food and who, in a submissive gesture, allows him or herself to be mounted by whom, are subtle signs of the hierarchy at work.

The mating season in late autumn is an important time for reassertions of social position. As the females come into oestrus, the exposed skin of the mature monkeys deepens in colour giving them bright scarlet bottoms and faces. The mating season attracts a number of male outcasts, a few of whom manage to infiltrate the troop and keep the incumbent males aggressively busy. A female forms a consort relationship with a male while she is in oestrus. Her single baby is born in spring and spends its first ten months extremely close to its mother. Sisters and daughters are fascinated by infants and they will groom the mother attentively, hoping to be allowed a glimpse of the baby or even to hold it.

As a general rule, young male macaques move to the periphery of the troop from the age of three and eventually leave. They may spend a number of years as loners before becoming accepted into another troop. Females remain in their natal troops and this is probably how incest is avoided. Thus, over the years, the troop's cohesion is maintained by matrilineal ties.

The versatile macaque troops have colonized further north than any other primate except man and have adapted to extreme conditions. In northern Honshu some live in areas where there is deep snow for four months of the year and have become known as the snow monkeys. Their coats are luxuriously thick and long, the outer hairs silvery white. In the Shiga Heights a few troops have found an ingenious method for keeping warm by bathing in the natural hot spring baths while flakes of snow fall on their heads. When they emerge the water on their hair quickly turns to a coat of ice. Foreigners who see this often exclaim that the shock of emerging into such bitter temperatures must ruin the pleasure of the bath but the Japanese know that the warmth from the natural hot spring stays with the macaques for many hours. At night, when the temperatures plummet, they make rough sleeping nests and huddle together for warmth.

Each morning soon after dawn the monkeys set off in search of food. The adults concentrate on feeding for roughly three sessions during the day. At other times they rest and groom each other while the youngsters play. Each troop uses a feeding area known as a home range which extends from 5 to 20 square km, depending on the size of the troop and the habitat.

The monkeys' diet consists of bark and winter buds as well as roots and tubers which they scrabble for under the snow. When the snow first arrives in Shiga Heights, some troops simply move across to the nearby ski resorts. While the youngsters tumble and toboggan in the snow, the adults supplement their winter diet by accepting scraps from tourists and foraging in rubbish bins.

In these northern deciduous forests the macaques have to travel further afield to find food than the monkeys in the evergreen forests of the southwest. Their diet alters with the changing seasons. When spring arrives their mainstay is shoots and leaves. The macaques are primarily herbivorous but will eat insects. Coastal monkeys supplement their diet with seafood such as shellfish. They also eat fruit, nuts, bark, buds and seeds when they are in season. One troop on Mount Hiei was recorded to feed from as many as 370 plant species over a year. In autumn they take both the young shoots of the mountain vegetables, which belong to the bracken family, and chestnuts from the

Snow monkeys bathing in the soporific yet invigorating natural hot spring baths at Jigokudani 'valley of hell' in the Shiga Heights.

Facing page: Careful grooming helps remove troublesome parasites but also has a social role in helping to maintain the cohesion of the troop. A study of thirteen individuals by Takeshi Furuchi showed that between 6 a.m. and 6 p.m. 23.4 per cent of their time was spent grooming.

forest floor, using their mobile lips to remove the hairy coat. They cram themselves with berries and pick mushrooms and other fungi from the lower tree trunks and the ground. In November the leaves finally drop and heavy snow begins to fall. While some troops, like those living in Shiga or further north in Shimokita, cannot escape the snow, others move down to the hills and valleys in search of food.

Each year the areas to which the monkeys travel are filled with more people. Today's tourist waiting in the 'autumn colour-viewing' queues to visit Nikko's yellow ginko trees or the blood-red maples in the Kyoto hills is easy prey for the monkeys. The macaques converge on the cars, halting the slow traffic. Some squat and groom in the middle of the road; others climb over the cars inspecting their occupants and begging for food. Squeals of delight turn to screams of fear and bellows of indignation as the monkeys steal purses or cameras, rummage through pockets, grab at food through open windows and snap angrily or bang on the car doors if thwarted. The people's love–hate relationship with the monkey is still in evidence. But both the monkeys' fortunes and the people's attitudes towards them

In early spring the macaques eat the buds, in May the blossoms and in July the fruit of the mountain cherry.

This road zig-zagging through Nikko National Park and famous for 'autumn colour-viewing' has the same number of curves as there are characters in the Japanese alphabet. Unwary tourists may find themselves suddenly surrounded by a macaque troop on the rampage for food.

Below: *Following a well-worn path, one macaque troop at Jigokudani in the Shiga Heights is on its way down to the feeding site. Through the winter their diet is supplemented three times a day.*

have been affected by a number of modern factors.

The monkey's mountain habitat has been eroded in the postwar drive to modernize and industrialize. Roads needed for forestry, hydro-electric dams and pylons have opened up previously isolated areas. Many of these were given national park status which encouraged sightseers. The tourist industry, in turn, created car parks, souvenir shops, hotels and viewing sites. With the philosophy that the national parks should provide recreation for a land-starved people, many appear to be little more than commercial playgrounds. Since much of the land within the parks is privately owned, management is extremely complicated. Only about 12 per cent of the national parkland (0.6 per cent of Japan's total land area) falls into the strictly protected category and even there the emphasis is on maintaining scenic beauty. Shiga Heights, home of the famous snow monkeys, consisted of one hotel and a few natural ski slopes before being designated a national park. It now has twenty-two ski resorts and 101 hotels.

If machines can now reach the highest peaks, traverse the deepest gorges, empty a mountain of its earth, lay pipes, power lines or ski runs across the most difficult terrain, then surely the reverence has gone and the Shinto gods have lost their sway. The loss of respect for mountains may profoundly affect the attitude to the monkey. If the mountains have lost their beauty, then they have lost their Shinto *kami* and they no longer need their monkey messengers.

Loss of habitat has a more direct and immediate effect on the monkeys. Vast areas have been displaced by commercial forestry. The Japanese have a healthy appetite for wood. Their houses are traditionally timber framed and the sliding screens which serve as doors are made of paper. Shrine buildings are regularly 'renewed' and after earthquakes there is a surge in the demand for timber, as after the 1923 devastation of the Tokyo region. Wood is required for paper manufacture and, of course, chopsticks, which are simply thrown away after fast-food meals. A campaign to persuade people to carry their own chopsticks

Protected for many years by the presence of so many shrines and temples, in the 1930s the forests of Nikko became one of Japan's earliest national parks. Away from the favoured tourist spots, the hills, stretching into the distance, are still home to macaque troops, black bears, Japanese serows, giant flying squirrels, racoon dogs and sika deer.

everywhere, in protest at Japan's drain on the world's rainforests, had little effect.

Japan still obtains 60 per cent of her timber from abroad and is the world's biggest importer of tropical hardwood logs. This seems excessive when her own forests cover 70 per cent of the land area, the highest proportion in the developed world, with 40 per cent under commercial plantation. The problem is essentially one of law and administration and it begins at home.

The displacement of natural woodland is the continuation of a process which began when the lowlands were first cleared for rice. Beech, the dominant deciduous forest type in the highlands, once covered 30 to 40 per cent of the land area. According to a recent Friends of the Earth report, estimates of the remaining primary beech forest (forest that has been left relatively unaffected by man) are as low as 1 to 5 per cent of the initial distribution. A third of the original primary forest has disappeared in the last thirty years. (By comparison, Britain, which has a similar forestry problem, lost 46 per cent of its semi-natural woodland between 1933 and 1983.) At the present rate of destruction the remaining Japanese primary beech forest could disappear in the next

Despite high mountain ranges and deep valleys, about 40 per cent of Japan's forest is commercially planted. Yet 60 per cent of her timber is still imported from abroad.

decade. But Japan, like Britain, still has official policies designed to increase commercial afforestation.

Before the mid 1900s beechwood was not exploited, except by charcoal burners, because it was considered unsuitable building material. Instead beech trees were cleared to create land space or replanted with cedar, cypress and larch. During the Second World War demand for these conifers increased, government funds were made available to plant them and beechwood was used for pulp, railway sleepers and housing material and was also found to be suitable for light aircraft. The Forestry Agency would normally have ploughed its profits back into the government pool but with forestry enjoying a postwar boom it opted to keep the revenue and invest it in planting more conifers. However, as western-style interiors and wooden furniture became fashionable (the Japanese house is traditionally uncluttered and without chairs) the demand for native beechwood increased, peaking in the 1960s.

Having replaced beechwood with conifers the agency had to look further afield for its supply. While new technology made the remote beech forests more accessible, the cost of road building, new machinery and wage increases began to put up the price of home-grown timber and buyers discovered they could get their wood more cheaply from abroad. The Forestry Agency is now sitting on a huge resource which is too expensive to harvest. Yet because it decided to keep its revenue, it is also having to cope with its losses. Wages must be paid and pensions maintained (company employees in Japan are looked after for life). The government still subsidizes the cost of planting, machinery and road building and, because of the pressure to retain jobs in rural areas, this policy is unlikely to change. The agency cannot afford to fell selectively as conservationists would wish because of the extra difficulties of labour and transportation; and it plants little beech because the trees take about a hundred years to reach maturity. Owners of private forests, have the same economic problems and so clearfelling and replanting with conifers continues.

The legacy is there for all to see. In the valleys and hills above the rice paddies and the houses there are always dark green conifers. In the mountains the ranks of planted trees stretch for many kilometres. It appears that more than 40 per cent of Japan's forest is in plantation because wherever there are roads, the foresters have been. As a result many native woodland plants and animals have become rare or extinct in the last forty years. The monocultures of planted trees allow few other species to colonize and have little to offer the native forest mammals

The uniformity of the single-species conifer plantation contrasts with the mosaic of autumn colour created by the variety of species in the native forests.

Facing page: *Japanese serow and calf. The serow is thought to be the closest living relative to the prehistoric ancestor of sheep and goats. It enjoys Japan's highest protected status, yet at the same time under licence it can be shot as a pest (see pages 197–9).*

such as the macaque, Asiatic black bear and Japanese serow.

The Japanese serow or kamoshika, found only in Japan, is an antelope-like goat related to the other serows of Asia. It has short curved horns, a goatlike face, cloven feet and a thick woolly coat. The serow is surefooted, capable of climbing rocky slopes or galloping fast across steep screes. It is shy and secretive, moving singly or in small groups, active in the cool of the day. One calf is normally born in June but the young from the previous year and even two-year-olds may follow their mother around. The serow, like the monkey, was once at home in the lowland forests before the land was taken over for rice cultivation and it was forced to live in higher altitudes. Now in summer it grazes on the alpine meadows but in winter the snow brings it down to the forests.

I first saw a Japanese serow in the distance, lying with a calf, well camouflaged at the foot of a tree in the mountains of Hakusan National Park. But during all my time in Japan I never saw a black bear. The same species as is found in forests across East Asia, it is often known as the crescent-moon bear because of the white band across its chest. Its diet is similar to that of the

macaque, although it eats fewer leaves and more nuts, fruit, berries and seeds. It opens ants' nests to feed on the ants and bees' nests for honey. In winter tree bark forms an important part of its diet.

Like the monkey, the bear and the serow have adapted their behaviour to cope with the loss of native forest. In winter serows nip the shoots off young cedar and cypress plants and black bears gnaw the bark in older plantations. This behaviour only adds to their problems since both are now hunted as pests. In addition, the medicinal qualities of the bear's gall bladder make shooting it a lucrative sport.

The black bear is one of seventeen land mammals, including forest creatures such as the badger-like racoon dog (*Nyctereutes procyonoides*) and the wild boar (*Sus scrofa*), which can be shot or captured with a game licence. Official figures from 1984 alone show that licences were issued to take 61,544 racoon dogs and 38,326 wild boar. The number of licensed hunters has increased to almost 500,000 since the 1950s.

The serow, whose numbers were thought to be as low as 3,000 in a rough estimate in 1935, has had special protection since

The Asiatic black bear is locally extinct in many areas. Between 1982 and 1984 2,848 were shot or captured during the hunting season and outside the season a further 3,107 were taken as pests.

1955 yet foresters, who blame it for damaging their trees, can obtain permission to shoot it as a pest (see page 197).

When the more resourceful monkey troops lose their traditional forest habitat they travel down beyond the plantations to find an alternative source of food. In rural villages over much of Japan monkeys are renowned for their ability to make lightning raids on orchards and vegetable crops. In a remote mountain region east of Tokyo a troop has been raiding since 1976 when a huge quarrying operation took a gigantic bite out of their mountain. The cunning monkeys always come at a different time of day and some days not at all. Converging *en masse* like an army, they devour everything in their path. They uproot vegetables from the fields, swarm over the village roofs to pinch fruits and soya beans drying outside the houses, and crowd the persimmon trees, gorging themselves on the ripe fruits and tossing the discarded ones to the ground. The raids generally last for about an hour unless the villagers arrive with sticks and stones to chase them away.

A popular fourteenth-century tale, 'The monkey and the crab', illustrates that monkeys have been raiding crops for hundreds of years:

> Once upon a time a monkey met a crab who was carrying a rice ball. The monkey wanted to eat the rice ball so he persuaded the crab to swap it for a persimmon seed. The crab planted the seed and tended it well and it grew into a large tree full of juicy persimmons. Being a crab he couldn't reach the persimmons so he asked his friend the monkey to help. The monkey agreed, but once in the tree he ate all the ripe persimmons and bombarded the crab with the hard green fruit. The crab was furious and asked his friends, a chestnut, a hornet, a kettle and a brick to help him take revenge on the monkey. They invited the monkey to tea. As he sat down, the chestnut jumped out of the fire and burnt him, then the kettle poured scalding water over him. The monkey screamed for help but the hornet flew in and stung him. As he raced out of the house, the brick fell off the roof and knocked him out!

Many such tales describe the monkey's cunning or evil deeds and the ensuing revenge taken. In the modern children's version of the story the monkey asks forgiveness, which is granted. He learns his lesson and does not try to steal again.

In reality crop raiding is on the increase. Both loss of habitat and provisioning have contributed to the problem. Monkeys were first fed or 'provisioned' by scientists in 1952, when

'Apes in a persimmon tree' by Mori Sosen (1747–1821) illustrates the story of the monkey who stole persimmons. With more than a third of the macaque population living close to farmland, 'engai' or monkey damage is an increasing problem. (The Toyama Kinekan Foundation)

primatologists encouraged the troops into open terrain in order to study their social behaviour. The increased confidence of the monkeys and their awareness that humans provide new sources of food has led to a higher incidence of crop raiding around provisioned sites. On Koshima Island, for example, where the monkeys are fed on the beach (see page 81), they discovered that they could cross to the mainland at low tide. A woman is hired to keep watch when the tide is out in an attempt to stop them. In Beppu volunteers patrol the crops at night. In Kyoto the sacred monkeys of Mount Hiei have begun raiding crops and emotions run particularly high. Attempts have been made to prevent them with firecrackers. In one area in the far north where farmers also have to cope with heavy snows, three out of four monkey troops were wiped out in retaliation in the early 1980s.

Licences to hunt monkeys can be obtained in areas where monkey damage is proven. Until 1968 permission was given by central government but when responsibility for this moved to the local town or village office the number of licences issued increased. Farmers have always had little patience for the animal

Mrs Iwamitsu, one of three women who take turns to guard the sandflats at low tide to stop the Koshima troop crossing to the mainland to raid crops. While she keeps watch she also collects and burns rubbish from the beach.

pests that steal their crops. However, the beliefs surrounding the monkey's powers presented farmers with a dilemma which, over the years, has protected it from being killed in many areas. Even today many farmers with hunting licences would rather trap monkeys than kill them. At one time zoos would take captured monkeys but they no longer need any more. A number continue to go to medical research establishments. Once people have permission to capture pest monkeys, there is no law which controls the animals' fate. Official figures show that each year approximately three thousand monkeys are captured, or shot and left to die.

Until there is a nationally coordinated plan to solve this problem the beleaguered farmers will continue to retaliate. In a survey of one of the problem areas 85 per cent of the people said they did not want the monkeys. Today roughly a third of the estimated population, ranging from 20,000 to 100,000 Japanese macaques, live in areas where they come into conflict with villagers, and with the present rate of habitat loss the situation can only worsen.

*   *   *

Like that of most of Japan's city dwellers my first view of Japanese macaques was of a monkey troop being provisioned. The monkeys are the subject of a scientific study on Koshima Island and a television crew was filming for a natural history quiz programme. As soon as the scientists arrived the first monkeys appeared on the beach, their noise alerting the rest of the troop. While the scientists counted them, the monkeys squabbled and screamed incessantly, cuffing and chasing each other and becoming especially vociferous when an intruder was sighted. The monkeys appeared to pick on certain victims and they also pestered tourists for food and mock charged cameras when they saw their reflections in the lenses.

The Koshima monkeys looked scrawny, shaggy and unkempt. A few of them had bald patches and were picking and scratching. In fact, all Japanese macaques look their worst in early spring. Their coats have lost the bright sheen of winter and they have begun to moult which causes them to groom obsessively. Their bodies are thin after the lean winter and tension is heightened because the females have just given birth.

The television crew was encouraging the monkeys to eat yoghurt from plastic cartons. When the scientists eventually fed them there was a mad scramble to grab the food and run. Nowadays, the monkeys are provisioned only four or five times a month so they were determined to get what they had come for.

Scientists have come and gone but Mrs Mito is still working with the Koshima macaques. She remembers Imo, the resourceful female macaque who first introduced potato washing to the troop. Imo is now dead but Mrs Mito remains close to her daughter.

Once it was learned that monkeys would accept food, they became a commercial proposition. Mount Takasaki near Beppu, for example, home of one of the first monkey troops to be successfully provisioned, is now a monkey park. In 1952 there were 220 individuals; now the population numbers over two thousand and the troop has split into three. One, with over a thousand members, may be the largest monkey troop in the world. Scientists have suggested that the concentrated nature of provisioned food and the larger troop size it supports generally increases the occurrence of aggression. Squabbling certainly seems to be the typical behaviour that is remembered by visitors to the monkey parks. As Professor Hirose has said, these monkeys have lost both their mystery and dignity.

Arashiyama monkey park overlooking Kyoto, one of Japan's thirty or so monkey parks which provide many citizens with their first glimpse of a wild macaque. At this park if the tourists want to feed the macaques they have to do so from inside a wired enclosure.

Japan has thirty or so monkey parks. Often included on city sightseeing tours, they are popular with tourists. An interesting experiment has been carried out for a number of years in Arashiyama monkey park in Kyoto. If tourists want to feed the monkeys they have to go inside a caged compound and buy fruit or nuts, which they can give to the monkeys, through wire netting. For once the humans are inside the cage and the monkeys outside. The visitors appreciate the irony and in this park the macaques no longer pester them. And in all monkey parks away from the feeding sites it is possible to observe brief cameos of typical monkey behaviour that would never occur in zoos. Tourists are fascinated to see monkeys drinking from pools, picking leaves, grubbing for insects, inspecting strange objects, sunbathing or fastidiously grooming each other. They laugh at the comical and bemused expressions as one young monkey loses a stick to a mischievous rival, or another takes a tumble in a rough game.

It has been said that there is more dilemma in the Japanese relationship with the monkey than with any other creature because of the similarities between monkey and man. Throughout history, drawing on their religious and artistic traditions, the Japanese have shown a remarkable ability to transfer their feelings and aspirations to the monkey. There are tales about monkeys who became believers in Buddha; and one implication of the three wise monkeys is that by avoiding evil, the monkeys will find enlightenment.

Sosen, the famous artist from the Edo period, painted endearing portraits of monkeys which capture the essential mobility in a monkey's face and express a whole gamut of 'human' emotions. According to legend he sketched from a captive monkey tethered in his garden. When people commented that the sketches did not look lifelike, he went into the mountains to study his subject in the wild. Sosen's paintings improved to such an extent that he was accused of painting his ancestors and was said to have turned from a monkey into a hermit. In later life Sosen appears to have accepted this argument, changing a character in his name into one meaning monkey.

Many years later when Japanese primatologists used the unique empathy with monkeys as a basis for their studies, they made some startling discoveries. In the 1950s and 1960s western scientists were using objective, rational and analytical methods to study primates, giving monkeys code names and avoiding anything that could be considered anthropomorphic. The Japanese were more subjective, and put the emphasis on the individual character of the monkeys. They spent years getting to know their monkeys, letting their behaviour rather than scientific rules dictate their findings.

One of the 'characters' was Imo, a female of high standing in the Koshima troop. The monkeys were provisioned with sweet potatoes and in 1953, when she was one year old, Imo discovered that if she took the yams to the water she could rub the mud off them. The behaviour gradually spread to her playmates, her mother and aunts. Later her own infants copied her and by the 1960s more than half the troop was potato washing; only the 'elders' from the preceding generation did not acquire the habit. The Koshima monkeys were also fed wheat grains, which the scientists buried in the sand to give them more time to study the monkeys. Once again the intelligent Imo learned that if she grabbed a mixture of wheat and sand and chucked it in the water the sand would drop and the floating wheat grains could easily be collected. This behaviour also spread following the same matrilineal pattern. Nowadays the monkeys are rarely fed

'Monkey and young with blue berries' by Mori Sosen (1747–1821). Sosen was celebrated for capturing the character of the macaque and for his use of delicate brushwork to convey the softness of its fur. (British Museum)

Macaque on Koshima Island eating a sweet potato. The discovery of potato washing in this troop disproved the theory that man was set above animals because only he had a culture.

wheat and many have forgotten the habit but a few infants still tiptoe out beyond their depth, blowing bubbles, as they try to eat the floating grains. Even though the potatoes now arrive scrubbed clean in plastic bags many monkeys still lollop to the sea to dunk them, perhaps because the habit is fixed or perhaps, as some scientists suggest, because they like the salty taste.

In an attempt to give a name to their methodology, the Japanese primatologists described their approach as 'kyokan' which translates as 'feel one' or sympathize with, an attitude they say comes naturally to them as Japanese. Western scientists criticized the early Japanese publications for being too anthro-pomorphic but since then both sides have met to discuss and share their ideas and long-term studies of individual primates, on the Japanese pattern, have become widespread. The findings at Koshima were hailed as a breakthrough in our understanding of the evolution of mankind. The Koshima monkeys put an end to the idea that man was set apart from animals because he had culture. Soon cultural customs within other animal societies were described. The initial discovery had, however, been made by a people whose indigenous religion, Shinto, did not subscribe to this difference between man and beast.

Man's biological and cultural proximity to the monkey was highlighted a few years later. Soon after the news that people had been horribly poisoned by eating fish contaminated with mercury, disturbing stories of crippled monkeys at monkey parks began to circulate. On Mount Takasaki the first deformed infant macaque was born two years after provisioning had started. By 1962 there were eight deformed monkeys. In 1970 10 per cent of the monkeys born were crippled. The luckier ones had their fingers joined; others had lost one limb or were born with none. Case histories were published – one population suffered frightening deformities a year after eating oranges which had been contaminated with a fluoride-based pesticide. Another troop was badly hit after the pregnant mothers ate apples that had been sprayed with a growth retardant, 2–4–5 T (to make them less susceptible to autumn typhoons). A third group of infants was affected after their parents drank water downstream from farm effluent.

The media caught on and photographs like those of children affected by the drug Thalidomide in the 1960s were widely displayed. Films were shown of disabled monkeys at parks and of a woman who attempted to bring up a deformed monkey in her home. Visitors to the parks witnessed the tenacity of the crippled monkeys, the support of close relatives and their remarkable capacity for survival. Some saw mothers trying to suckle hopelessly deformed and even dead infants, refusing to let anyone take them away. The images struck particularly hard at the hearts of pregnant women who feared that similarly contami-nated fruit and vegetables would affect their unborn children. Ecologists warned that one in every five babies in Japan could be born deformed. In fact the situation never became so grave and more stringent controls on pesticides were introduced. Park keepers were warned of the danger and the incidence of crippled monkeys in monkey parks fell. But the scenes had given new force to the Japanese empathy with monkeys.

At Arashiyama monkey park the local primary schoolchildren have formed a friendship society. Their friends are the monkeys. They spend hours watching and occasionally drawing while the monkeys move unconcernedly among them. The children can recognize individual monkeys, calling them by name and picking out favourites. They record their observations and contribute to detailed charts placed inside the visitors' cage which describe the histories of individual monkeys.

The understanding of monkeys was strengthened by a recent discovery at Arashiyama. In 1979 a three-year-old female monkey was seen to play with stones. Gradually, other members began

During holidays and weekends these children spend hours observing this troop at Arashiyama, contributing information to various scientific studies.

'Stone play' was first recorded as a new cultural behaviour in 1979. Play is thought to have an important role in the initiation of new behaviour and it is not surprising that stone play, like potato washing, was first observed in young macaques.

to 'stone play' and by 1983 it was commonplace. At their feeding site – an open area covered sparsely with loose gravel – the monkeys sit on the ground collecting piles of stones. Some concentrate on gathering a number of stones and mixing them up, while others roll one stone, follow it and pick it up again. While I was watching, rubbing or clacking the stones together seemed to be popular. Adults and young hug stones to their chest and carry them to rough ground to play in seclusion, but other monkeys often steal their stone pile and they have to start again. Stone playing normally occurs after feeding so it is unlikely that, like begging for instance, it has been conditioned by a feeding reward. Also, it is occasionally practised at other times of the day. Scientists have not been able to explain stone play in terms of direct benefit or adaptive value to the monkeys. It may be a way of easing the tension created by the artificial situation of over a hundred monkeys crowded together at feeding time. But it seems more relevant to conclude that like the schoolchildren, the monkeys simply enjoy playing.

An example of monkey behaviour that is startling to witness, perhaps because the monkey behaves so like a human, is the performance of the monkey player. In the days when people believed that monkeys had curative powers, medicine men travelled round Japan with a monkey on a rope. Their popularity increased among the horse-owning samurai when the belief that monkeys could cure livestock became current. Some taught their monkeys tricks with which to amuse their clientele and the transformation from curative to performing monkey took place. Monkey performances were a popular folk art in the Edo period and some were patronized by the aristocracy and invited to perform in their homes.

The monkey showman has recently been revived by the descendants of a monkey trainer of the Edo period. The training procedure and performance is said to be true to that of Edo days. The heyday of the monkey player occurred when rules about Japanese etiquette and manners were most strictly adhered to. This is reflected in the monkey's performance. His posture and behaviour towards his master is extremely important. The monkey walks on his hind legs with his back as straight and stiff as a ramrod. Discipline is strict and if he misbehaves he reacts to his master's voice as if he has been stung. Yet he somehow manages to bow in Japanese fashion and show obeisance without humbling himself. In deference to modern times he is also trained to sit upright in a chair. The monkey manages to perform acrobatic tricks, walking on stilts and jumping through hoops, at the same time maintaining an

The monkey showman and his monkey are constant companions and their performance draws appreciative crowds all over Japan. Eye contact is aggressive behaviour in macaque society and to establish his dominance in the early days of training the trainer has to outstare his monkey.

Below: *An* inro, *a decorative container for pills and medicines, once part of traditional Japanese dress. (By courtesy of the Board of Trustees of the Victoria & Albert Museum)*

arrogant and supercilious expression. The trainers claim that success in teaching the monkey to behave like a human depends on treating them like humans.

When questioned about their attitude towards the monkey, many Japanese refer to the Shinto belief that monkeys are on the same plane as humans. One girl spoke of watching the monkey show and feeling sorry for the monkey, then thinking that perhaps it was happier and prouder than wild monkeys because it could perform tricks. This reveals the remarkable ability to project personal feelings on to an animal, yet it indicates clearly that applying human emotions to monkeys is not always to the monkey's advantage. Others refer to the monkey as a cunning trickster (a legacy from the many local tales that grew around the monkeys who stole crops). To most city people the monkey is either a 'cute' creature or the animal they have seen in a monkey park. Some people mentioned the three wise monkeys, saying that their desire to conform matches the Japanese mentality. Nobody, apart from some primatologists and conservationists, mentioned the wild monkey and its loss of habitat. One conservationist, referring to the modern destruction of the Japanese landscape, said sardonically, 'The three wise monkeys are about closing your senses to, or ignoring, what you don't want to know.'

It is impossible to believe that the people cannot see the destruction of their landscape and its effect on the monkey, bear, serow and other wildlife. It may simply be that, in the tremendous economic drive, most people see the development of the land as a sign of progress rather than an ugly replacement of natural habitat. Yet some people have taken their hands from their eyes and begun to speak out. Against the sentiment of the seven-monkey poem they are questioning what is happening to their land. At the Japan monkey centre I was shown some wise monkeys doing what they are not supposed to do. In one trio the first monkey listened to a radio, the second bellowed down a loudspeaker, while the third watched through a pair of binoculars.

Of all the large mammals, the monkey can be seen most easily in the wild and it may therefore help more people, like the children who spend their spare time at Arashiyama monkey park, decide that for modern Japan their wildlife *still* has value.

Modern and irreverent interpretations of the three wise monkeys.

AS THE CHERRY BLOSSOMS FALL

If there was no such thing
As cherry blossoms
In this world
In Springtime how untroubled
Our hearts would be!

A ninth-century poem by Ariwara no Narahira
translated by Paul Berry and Celeste Adams

In the words of the famous wandering poet Basho: 'The first lesson for the artist is . . . to follow nature, to be at one with nature.' In all its varied moods nature is the tapestry and inspiration from which many Japanese artists have drawn to reflect on and describe human emotions. The elegant simplicity of ikebana or flower arranging, the refinement of the tea garden, the effortless grace of the dances named after flowers or birds, the flow from painter through brush and ink to paper – all reveal the oneness of man with the raw materials of nature.

One of the oldest surviving examples of artistic creativity in Japan began with the introduction of wet rice cultivation from China, when, with little flat land suitable for agriculture, the people began to ditch and terrace the hills, creating new landscapes. Over the centuries, as new cultivation techniques reached them, the Japanese farmers became adept sculptors. The land they fashioned was gentle, aesthetic and decoratively pleasing and it remained so for hundreds of years until the Meiji restoration.

Glimmers of this traditional landscape are still found in the mapped precision of rice shoots, the rows of carefully pruned peach, pear or apple trees and the humped tea bushes set against the vertical poles of conifer or bamboo plantations. Neatly stepped terraces climb the hills, a bank or wall enclosing each tiny paddy field. Looking down on the valleys in spring is

like looking into a honeycomb. After the harvest the fields are patterned with sheaves of drying rice straw, as if an artist had chosen to fill each cell with a different design. Some farmers make small stooks, building them up into huts, some pyramidal, some with umbrella-like roofs. Some lay the sheaves out flat to dry, bound at one end like fans, while others lash wooden poles together and drape the straw over them. The houses are surrounded by lines and patterns: persimmons bobbing on string by the door; log piles; stones in the wall; squid or soya beans hanging on trellises; stacks of oyster shells and tidy rows of leeks or radishes.

The careful asymmetric patterning in the agricultural landscape blends with the natural backdrop: the stands of cedar, the curve of the hills, and particularly the dormant volcanic cones. Fujisan reflected in the water of a rice paddy dappled with the squares of the planted shoots, or the bowl of an old volcano rising above a scarf of mist, framed by dark green conifers, are perfect compositions. One could argue that such visual pleasure is brought about by chance or economic necessity but the effect is so precisely achieved that I believe that this landscape is the earliest manifestation of the Japanese mastery of design.

When the Japanese became farmers they removed wildlife from their doorstep. Yet they still, of course, relied on nature to provide the rain and sunshine to grow their crops. Many of the traditional Shinto *matsuris* or festivals are associated with agricultural rites. The nature *kami* are invoked and thanked for the good things they have provided. And they are entertained by a variety of art forms including dance.

The earliest dances were thought to be lively and spontaneous and were said to originate from the myth of creation. The sun goddess, offended by her brother, hid in a cave and plunged the world into darkness. The other heavenly deities hatched a plot to draw her out. One, the 'dread female of heaven', danced suggestively outside and the others burst into ribald laughter. Overcome with curiosity the sun goddess peeped out and light returned to the world.

Over the years the festivals have changed and the dances have been influenced by the cultural traditions of China and other countries. The butterfly and nightingale dances, performed in sumptuous costumes at shrines like Ise or Iwashimizu Hachiman are dreamy and gentle in mood. Others, particularly

Neat banks of mud attempt to hold the water in each tiny paddy field. In a country where flat land is in short supply, every reclaimable metre is put to economic use.

those in rural areas, are wild and exciting like the cuckoo dance in which young men scatter artificial blossoms as they leap into the air in appreciation of the profusion of flowers in spring. Some dances, such as the cherry blossom one in spring or the praying mantis in early summer, symbolize seasons; others like the white heron and lion dances performed at the summer Gion festival in Kyoto, are thought to drive away plague and pestilence. The deer dances in Shikoku or the jumping frog dance in Nara prefecture are based on ancient tales and legends. In each the emotion of the dancers is conveyed through the movements of the animal or bird.

*   *   *

It is in poetry, however, that the Japanese use of wildlife to express their emotions is more clearly evident. A passion for nostalgia and sadness is a sensibility unique to the Japanese. This feeling for the pathos of life is described by the Japanese word *aware*. The pathos is refined, sensitive and artistic, a state of mind which encourages an awareness of and sympathy with nature's changing moods. Nature is the ideal raw material for poets wishing to evoke the melancholy spirit of *aware*. The attitude towards nature is not so much one of love as subjective sympathy. The artist is attracted to the nuance of mood, the fragility and the uncertainty in nature which seems to reflect the human lot.

Five qualities together describe traditional Japanese poetry,

The Miyako dance, performed by geisha girls in the ancient capital Kyoto, celebrates the gift of spring.

the first being this love of wistfulness and nostalgia. The second is the importance of the poem's mood. The Japanese language allows subtle changes of mood, many of which are lost in translation. The third is the ordinariness or earthiness of the subject matter. Poets writing in Japanese were generally more interested in real and homely things and events, whereas those writing in Chinese were more concerned with religion and politics. The fourth is muted suggestion. A veil hangs over Japanese poetry. Descriptions are brief, leaving much to the imagination and complete poems are short and fleeting. The most consistent Japanese styles are the *waka*, using thirty-one syllables in five-line stanzas, and latterly the *haiku* which allows only seventeen syllables. The fifth is the use of imagery from nature, one of the most consistent and appealing qualities of Japanese poetry.

Nature is the perfect medium for conveying the other four attributes: for instance, melancholy reflection and mood in the following poems from the late Heian period:

> *A man without feelings*
> *Even, would know sadness*
> *When snipe start from the marshes*
> *On an autumn evening.*

And:

> *At my side*
> *Autumn weed-flowers*
> *Whisper softly –*
> *'How dear to me*
> *Are all things that die.'*

Ordinariness and earthiness are evident in the interest in life in its lowliest form, as in this poem by Kobayashi Issa (1763–1827) and the folk song which follows it:

> *For fleas, also, the night*
> *Must be so very long,*
> *So very lonely.*

> *When summer comes,*
> *The paddy pools grow warm*
> *The mudloach and the singing frog*
> *Are happy, happy,*
> *Thinking they're in a bath.*

Muted suggestion is conveyed by a dawn mist, shadows, the summer rains, falling snow, the dim light of the moon or the calling of a hidden animal or bird, as in this poem from the late Heian period:

The cuckoo called:
I looked towards the sound,
But only the moon
Of the dawn was there.

Traditional Japanese poetry is also said to have four recurring themes: love, parting, the seasons and nature. Again nature is ideally suited to evoke the first three. Time, particularly its passing as in the Buddhist transience of life or the Shinto passion for the changing seasons, is illustrated by fading flowers or dying leaves. An empress recited the following poem in the fourth century as she longed for her departed lover:

In the autumn field,
Over the rice ears,
The morning mist trails,
Vanishing somewhere . . .
Can my love fade too?

A sense of whimsy creeps in to many Japanese poems particularly when animals are used to reflect human situations as in this seventeenth-century poem by Basho, the poet who named himself after a banana tree:

Winter's first rain
Monkey needs
A raincoat too.

With the Japanese delight in playing on words nature was given two other important roles in poetry. Pillow words, descriptive words which qualified a noun or concept, were devised in the sixth century. For instance a woman's hair might be described by the leopard flower which is black. Yamato, the old name for Japan, was qualified by Island of the Dragonfly. The ring formed by mating dragonflies, reminiscent of the ring of mountains which surrounded the early Yamato, is thought to be the inspiration for this pillow word. Much of the flowery evocativeness of early poetry was lost when the *waka* forced strict limitations on the number of syllables and pillow words died out because they were too long.

As poetry became even more suggestive and symbolic, seasonal words were developed. These were used in a game in which a group of poets linked verses, keeping subjects such as flowers or the moon strictly within the correct season. From this the *haiku* developed. One can guess the season from the scene or mood evoked in the following examples:

> *Soon it will die*
> *But no trace of this*
> *In the cicada's screech . . .*

refers to the ending of summer. The phrase, 'they have learned to live in a land without flowers' and the following poem refer to the wild geese who, because they scorn the cherry blossom, flying northwards away from it, signify spring.

> *Dumplings before cherries*
> *He says, and back he goes,*
> *The wild goose.*

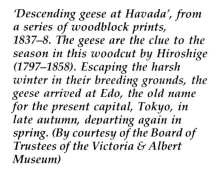

'Descending geese at Havada', from a series of woodblock prints, 1837–8. The geese are the clue to the season in this woodcut by Hiroshige (1797–1858). Escaping the harsh winter in their breeding grounds, the geese arrived at Edo, the old name for the present capital, Tokyo, in late autumn, departing again in spring. (By courtesy of the Board of Trustees of the Victoria & Albert Museum)

Geese arriving would signify autumn, as would the harvest moon, the cry of the curlew, and the rice stubble left behind after the harvest.

Poetry remains a national pastime and poems continue to be

inspired by nature. The season game is still played, as shown by a recent anthology which lists over 4,600 season words. Some, such as 'windsurfing' are modern, but many still depend on wildlife. The game must originally have encouraged the poets to study nature but, once the season words had become part of a convention, they could be exploited for art; exploited because there was no need to look at or take account of natural phenomena in order to use them as symbols and metaphors. The richness of nature was the poets' source of inspiration and they turned nature into symbols. But their art did not depend on caring for nature in the wild. In the sense of the words of a poet from the Heian period: 'When we hear the notes of the nightingale among the blossoms, when we hear the frog in the water, we know that every living being is capable of song.' The poets in the Shinto sense considered wild things to be their equal and, by simple extension, believed that nature shared their emotions.

*   *   *

The expression of the emotions was also a strong feature of Japanese paintings and birds, flowers and animals are central to various styles. Japan's debt to Chinese art is readily acknowledged and it was not until the Heian period, after two centuries of absorbing ideas from China and Korea, that a Japanese, as opposed to Chinese style of art began to emerge. The *Tale of Genji*, the most celebrated example of court literature, written around the year 1007 is filled with references to nature and describes an elegant and pleasurable existence. The court aristocrats looked to nature to share or inspire their emotions. They walked under fruit blossoms, glided in boats down the river, viewed the moon with a loved one, and watched the autumn colours seep slowly through the maples, from yellow to orange and rust and finally a deep blood red.

The language of the court paid homage to the ephemeral beauty of wild flowers which suited both the gentle spirit of *aware* and the prevailing Buddhist notions of the transience of life. Their names were given to palace rooms and were used to distinguish between ranks. Flowers described the colour or lining of garments and a change of clothes signalled each new season. In spring the nobles wore the colours of willow and cherry blossom, in summer azalea, in autumn clover and white chrysanthemum, and in winter, pine. The *Tale of Genji* speaks of the dances of the spring lark and of the willow and flower garden. The total picture is of refined, languishing and artistically creative men and women. Yet their glimpses of nature were carefully selected; nobles sent to the provinces wrote of uncouth

Facing page: 'Mount Fuji from Lake Ashi in Hakone', a woodblock print by Katsushika Hokusai (1760–1849). Poems often accompany Japanese paintings and here the mood, carefully attained using graphic simplicity and a select choice of colour, is enhanced by the inclusion of two haikus: 'The dancing skylarks/Compare the height of their voices/To the tall peak' (Keika); 'The foothills of Mt Fuji in the Spring/Are covered with mist/Like the pattern of a ceremonial gown' (Nikyō). (Chester Beatty Library)

舞雲雀
声も
高根と
丈くらべ

桂花

熨斗目ほと
霞む裾野や
春きぬ不二

二橋

'Moonlit night at the Suehiro bridge, Tempōzan, Osaka', by Yashima Gakutei (1786–1868). Viewing the moon with a loved one was a popular pastime for courtiers in the Heian period. That artists continue to depict these themes indicates the importance of the contemplation of nature to the Japanese. (British Museum)

wild places and pined for the sanctuary of the court. Within this closed domain teams discussed the rival merits of living things or art objects. They played this game with painted stones, shells, flowers, insects and even spiders. And, similarly, they cast judgment over paintings. Out of this came *Yamato-e* which, literally translated, means Japanese pictures.

Yamato-e shared one characteristic common to all oriental art: a rich expression of nature. The great age of flower and bird paintings was the three hundred years of the Sung Dynasty which began in 960. These faithful but formal representations of nature were highly regarded in Japan but the Japanese are generally accredited with putting more emotion and more human elements into their art than the more formal Chinese who directed their artistic imagination towards learning and philosophy. In Japan, as the overall mood of a painting was considered more important than reality, more thought was given to decoration and composition. Whereas in a Chinese painting flowers and birds were generally positioned in their correct context, in Japanese paintings they could be free. The artist whose work was imbued with imagination and emotion was more highly praised than one who copied faithfully from the external world.

In later years, when strict rules of etiquette dictated behaviour, the artist was one of the few in society whose individual freedom of expression was encouraged. The whirling patterns of flowers and the colours of bird feathers made both ideally suited to design. Birds were also useful because their ability to fly enabled the artist to place them anywhere within the composition. Flowers and birds were also used decoratively on clothing, utensils and gifts.

Yamato-e was pretty. Thin lines were filled with thick paints coloured with natural pigments to create flat images lacking light and shade. The paintings were carefully asymmetric, the mood gentle and refined. Above all the compositions were decorative, revealing the strong Japanese sense of design. For

'A flight of cranes', embroidered in silks and gold thread on satin for a **fukasa** *(gift cover) of the Edo period. After Sotatsu painted his thousand cranes, one for each year of their legendary life, in the seventeenth century the multi-crane motif became popular. (By courtesy of the Board of Trustees of the Victoria & Albert Museum)*

themes, *Yamato-e* was strongly influenced by Japanese life and literature and a painting would often accompany a poem. Painters in the native tradition concentrated on everyday or secular subjects such as fishermen drying their nets, people out at a picnic or playing literary games. Each painting indicated a time of year; the sites visited by courtiers to view cherry blossoms or the seven grasses of autumn were popular subjects. That the Japanese continued to depict these themes through the Edo period and still gather to witness these events, is evidence of the special hold the changing seasons have always had over the Japanese soul.

Humour is also a theme of Japanese art. Some scrolls survive from the twelfth century in which people were caricatured as animals. Monkeys, deer, rabbits and frogs are portrayed at leisure, picnicking, rowing, and playing games. They are thought to have been painted by Buddhist monks as a mark of their disgust at the dissolute ways of the aristocracy. Portraits of

Chōjū Giga ('Frolicking animals'), handscroll, ink on paper from the twelfth century. The depiction of animals acting in human roles was probably intended as a form of protest against the permissive court society and a mockery of Buddhist ritual. (Kozan-ji, Kyoto)

animals were often whimsical. In the Edo period, it became popular to use animals in thinly disguised social satire to comment on human traits. In some pictures animals were simply given human faces or expressions. Sometimes the result is comic, at other times more serious, but it takes to extremes the use of animals to express emotion or mood.

Whilst *Yamato-e* or the Japanese style developed in some schools, others developed along Chinese lines. From China, for example, came the art of painting with brush and black ink known as *sumi-e*. Oriental art has always been admired for its expression by the use of simple lines, of the way in which an animal or plant moves or grows. This ability to give life to subjects has been explained by the freedom of the flexible brush as opposed to a hard quill or pen to draw outlines. Perhaps, however, it has more to do with the tradition of painting animals subjectively rather than copying them from the external world. In China the subjectivity was based on a scholarly,

'Night heron' by Shūgetsu, a sumi-e painting in which a few carefully chosen brushstrokes convey the character and purposeful movement of the stalking heron. (School of African and Oriental Studies)

philosophical attitude. In Japan, which was more romantic, less rational and more emotional in its approach to art, it was easier to incorporate human feelings.

The introduction of Zen from China had a profound effect on ink painting. In tune with the traditions of Shinto, Zen encouraged people to go out and contemplate nature. They painted not what they saw but the intensity of their own experience. In his book *Zen and the Fine Arts*, Shin'ichi Hisamatsu says that Zen was typified not by realism or symbolism but by expressionism. For the Zen monks the external world was a pool of inspiration with which to express man's infinite depths. Tranquillity, serenity, brevity and space or nothingness were important concepts which the monks transferred to their paintings. The genius of Zen-inspired *sumi-e* is that a few lines painted in black ink sparkle with life. Allusion and suggestion are taken to their limits yet the painter still manages to depict, with a few brushstrokes, the sparrow fluttering by the lithe bamboo or the egret stalking through the reeds. A bird was either lively or drooping, about to fly away or catch something, a monkey arrogant or inquisitive, a bamboo resilient but flexible in the face of a storm.

With so many subjective uses of nature it is not surprising that in the orient so many wildlife forms became symbols. In China, plum, the first tree to bloom after the winter snows, was a symbol of longevity and courage. The association with longevity linked it with bamboo and pine to complete 'the three friends'. All three symbolized antiquity and scholarly endurance in the face of adversity, the plum for bringing a breath of spring, the bamboo for enduring the harsh winter winds through its flexibility and the pine through its strength.

In Japan the symbols were more widely interpreted and linked more directly with human emotions. The plum, like the cherry blossom, which in Japan has a brief period of opulence before an April shower or a strong breeze takes the blooms, became a nostalgic symbol of all that is ephemeral. Plum and cherry also brought hope and happiness. Morning glory was a popular illustration of the transience of life: blooming in splendour at midday, by evening it has faded. The nightingale (actually a bush warbler) sang for summer and happiness. Crows were synonymous with filial piety because the young were thought to look after their ageing parents. (In fact the parents chase the young away as soon as they are ready to breed again.) The sparrow symbolized smallness, happiness and friendship. With the bamboo it became a popular couplet, denoting an accommodating and tolerant friendship. The

'A pair of mandarin ducks', emblems of conjugal felicity. The flowering peony, a symbol of opulence, highlights the contrast between the gorgeous drake and the drab female to which he remains faithful. Fan design by Kitao Shigemasa (1738–1819). (By courtesy of the Board of Trustees of the Victoria & Albert Museum)

mandarin drake personified conjugal happiness because, despite his finery, he never leaves the drab, brown female.

The carp as a symbol of courage and ambition is believed to date back to a legendary tale of a carp that climbed a waterfall, although carp are not known to 'leap' like salmon. Today on every 5 May, which is known traditionally as Boys' Day, painted carp streamers flutter like windsocks above the houses of male children. At the Meiji shrine in Tokyo children write their hopes on a paper carp which swims in the breeze.

Although some artists who painted symbols kept animals in captivity, it is generally agreed that they spent little time sketching wildlife from nature. Those who did were noted in historical writings because they were unusual. For so many artists the

'Carp swimming among waterweeds' by Katushika Taito, Edo period. As a symbol of courage, the carp's strength is conveyed by the coloured bands of water through which it passes. Taito's design is thought to have been prompted by a poem by Bumbunsha: 'It turns into a dragon, shows its strength, the carp that enters the cloud of flowers reflected in the Sumida River.' (Chester Beatty Library)

symbol was more important than the reality. The continual repetition of incongruous themes – carp climbing waterfalls, pine with plum and bamboo, cranes standing on turtles, a rabbit riding in the moon – also suggest that natural accuracy was irrelevant. It was more important that animals matched in the world of symbols, where they evoked certain moods. Even animals and plants which were readily observable became repeatedly stylized. Pine trees and flying plovers, for example, are difficult to identify by someone unfamiliar with their conventional representation.

The Japanese also adopted plants and animals as symbols from China although they did not occur naturally in Japan. The lion (the Asiatic lion still survives in India) was king of a hundred animals. A legend in which lions were revitalized by eating peonies is thought to be the origin of a popular couplet which found particular favour with the samurai. Both tigers and gibbons were copied from Chinese paintings, the gibbon a symbol of grief and the tiger, linked with bamboo, to portray strength with flexibility. The Japanese could only copy or work from skins so it is hardly surprising that they painted oddly proportioned tigers with strange grimaces or gibbons with arms too short for their bodies.

The Japanese artists also used the twelve animal symbols from the Chinese Taoist system of counting and dating. In addition to the dragon, they accepted other mythological creatures such as the phoenix and the kirin, which is a cross between a lion and a dragon.

Japanese painters had then a tremendous range of animal symbols to call on. Yet in so many cases they joined a school and simply copied the work of their masters. As one artist explained, 'These symbols already have a place in the people's heart; there is no need to go and search for them in the wild.' None the less the foundations of a realistic portrayal from nature were laid down in the sixteenth century. Before Japan closed her doors at the beginning of the Edo period new influences were absorbed from China and Portugal. Two schools which used flowers and birds as their principal subject matter stand out: the Rimpa school guided by Koetsu, Sotatsu and Korin, and the earlier Kano school which traditionally passed from father to son. Both

'Tigers in a bamboo grove', a painted screen of the Kano school. These grumpy tigers, linked with bamboo in a popular couplet, symbolize strength with flexibility. The artist would not have seen living tigers; his inspiration would have been taken from copies of Chinese paintings and perhaps a tiger skin. (By courtesy of the Board of Trustees of the Victoria & Albert Museum)

styles were simple, yet extremely decorative, with a clear emphasis on composition. Kano painters expressed themselves across the large sliding paper screens in the houses of the aristocracy. Both schools used gold, a colour obviously alien to nature, and freely mixed plants and animals which were not found together naturally. They were also extremely versatile and in preparation for their work many appear to have filled sketchbooks with studies of nature. For artists like Korin examples remain to prove this.

Okyo Maruyama (1733–95) founded the Maruyama school, the first 'school' of 'wildlife artists' in the western sense. He urged his pupils to make detailed studies of birds, plants and insects from the wild. The artists did not confine themselves to conventions or couplets but sketched what they saw: maple, wistaria and willow; persimmons, chestnuts and radishes. Some of Maruyama's sketches have recently been collected and published. They are remarkable for their scientific accuracy. In his sketches of songbirds, for example, the feather tracts are relatively – and unusually – correct.

The English illustrator Joseph Wolf (1829 – 99) is considered by some naturalists and wildlife artists to have been the first to combine the accurate sketching of feather tracts with pictures of birds that actually looked as though they could fly away. Yet Maruyama's work predates Wolf's by about a hundred years. He would have seen the much admired Dutch style of naturalist painting which reached Japan by its only open port, Nagasaki. But typically these were stiff, profiled portraits, clearly suggesting stuffed animals or skins. Maruyama's work stands out because it combines realistic portrayal with life and grace. His birds and insects actually look as if they would leap off the page if one touched them. Perhaps Japanese artists led the way because Zen had taught them how to distil a subject to its essential character and they had traditionally put 'life' in the form of human emotions into their arts.

*   *   *

The importance of mood and emotion is evident in many other Japanese arts. Shinto, Zen and Taoist influences found common ground in the use of nature to express man's place on the earth.

In the ninth century a Buddhist brought to Japan the seeds of the tea plant, which is whipped into a bitter pea-green broth in the tea ceremony. This was originally drunk by Chinese monks as an aid to meditation but the 'way of tea', developed in the fifteenth century, was entirely Japanese. Zen brought the *wabi*, the importance of rustic simplicity, to tea drinking. The careful,

Detailed studies of a Siberian meadow bunting by Okyo Maruyama (1733–95). In Japanese painting a decorative and careful design was usually more important than fidelity to nature. Maruyama, who encouraged his pupils to make detailed studies from nature, is credited as the founder of naturalism in Japanese painting. (The Tokyo National Museum)

'Teahouse over a stream', fan design by Ando Hiroshige (1797–1858). 'The stream continues to flow but it is not the same water', was written in the twelfth century by Kamono Chomei. The tea-garden was designed to create a tranquil atmosphere, an ideal setting for contemplation. (By courtesy of the Board of Trustees of the Victoria & Albert Museum)

simplistic design of the tea-room and tea-garden and the slow ritual of serving tea created a tranquil atmosphere. All the Zen-inspired arts are characterized by brevity, asymmetry, and the suggestion of hidden depths – filling in the missing gaps may help one on the road to self-awareness.

Under the patronage of the tea ceremony the arts of pottery, ikebana and creating tea-gardens flourished. Flower arranging is a pastime which some trace back to the custom of dedicating flowers to the Buddha and others to the offering of evergreen branches to the nature *kami*. Ikebana, a special type of arrangement created to fill an alcove and elevate the mind to the contemplation of beauty, was essential to the atmosphere of the tea-room. Ikebana differs strikingly from western flower arrangements in that it does not concentrate on exotic plants or flowers in full bloom. Instead the arranger seeks out buds, grasses, wood and leaves. Blighted buds or dying leaves express the ephemerality of life. Once the buds have opened or the leaves turned, the mood of the arrangement changes and the artist must start afresh. Ikebana requires even more cutting and trimming than other flower arrangements because brevity, suggestion and asymmetry are so important. Each cut requires sensitivity and concentration. Material is bent, twisted and coaxed into the desired shape. Flowers like chrysanthemums are sometimes backed petal by petal with thin wire to ensure the required shaping of each blossom. The use of branches and buds in preference to flowers in full bloom, the emphasis on naturalism and the asymmetry of nature and the use of seasonal flowers have suggested to some that ikebana is popular because it re-creates wild nature in the home. In fact ikebana is an art which simply uses nature to create a required design and mood. Nature is its inspiration rather than its aim. It provides a medium for those all over the world who practise ikebana to express their mood and their originality.

Japanese gardens are also often described as re-creations of nature. The introductory leaflet to Kenrokuen in Kanazawa, one of Japan's most famous landscape gardens, reads: 'Trees, flowers, stones, paths and streams should be represented as they appear in nature. The idea is to live in harmony with nature, not to conquer it, as seems to be the tendency in the more artificial gardens of other countries.' Kenrokuen is beautiful: alongside cherries and maples planted in a carpet of moss, water flows under bridges and in and out of ponds and lakes. Early in the morning before the tourists come, only Kenrokuen's many gardeners are at work, making sure that not a blade of wild nature rests or grows where it is not wanted. On a visit in autumn, I watched a group of ten or so gardeners sitting on little wooden stools in the stream, picking up and wiping each stone clean. In front of them the stones, jumbled and confused by the current, wore a green haze of algae. Behind them, neatly placed and glossy, the stones sparkled in the sunlight.

At a nearby Zen temple I saw trainee monks, wearing the white towelling headcloths typical of the working man, busy raking the leaves and pruning the carefully rounded azalea bushes. In Kyoto and elsewhere, whenever I visited a Japanese garden I found people forever sweeping, raking, shaping and pruning, giving real nature no more of a chance than in the formal western garden.

Some Zen gardens are devoted solely to the contemplation of rocks and moss or a few stones laid carefully in a bed of raked sand or gravel. These stone gardens take the Zen themes of brevity and austerity to new limits. Yet, in the quiet surrounds

Men and women brushing stones in the Kenrokuen gardens in Kanazawa. They are removing the algae from each stone and neatly replacing them to give a more pleasing effect. Wild nature is given no more chance to flourish in a Japanese garden than in a formal western garden.

of a temple, suggestion is still strong; the rocks could be mountains, the raked patterns on the sand, flowing water. In Japan today where space is at a premium, such a garden, the size of a tatami mat, a mere 90 × 180 cm, might be found in the middle of a conference room or at the entrance to a hotel. In these gardens it seems that in the spirit of Zen's desire to take away the clutter from the mind, all the unwanted debris is removed. Nature remains only in symbolic form and the garden has become pure, abstract, subjective design.

Bonsai, the art of training a tree to grow into a particular shape in miniature, was introduced to Japan from China at around the same time as Zen but its beginnings lie in Taoism. The tree was said to express the harmony between heaven, earth and man. Although man turns something natural into a miniature artefact, he can only do so by recognizing the intrinsic growth pattern of the tree. Bonsai eventually spread among the ordinary people and, like ikebana, maintains its popularity today in cities, far removed from wild trees and flowers. I met businessmen, factory workers and priests whose hobby was bonsai. Over the tens of years, during which they remain in one family, bonsai are pampered, pruned and 'disciplined' to grow

This miniature garden, which enhances the tranquil and contemplative atmosphere of a tea house in Kyoto, is inspired by the Zen themes of brevity, austerity and implicit suggestion.

Below: *As he disciplined his* **bonsai** *with soft wires Kensho Ohta, a priest, explained that he had learned to respect that each section of the tree had its own world or privacy.*

Facing page: *The ruddy kingfisher comes to Japan to breed in the spring. Captured on film by Tadashi Shimada in Hokkaido, it is a beautiful example of the merit of seeking perfection in whatever medium an artist chooses.*

in certain shapes. Much has been written about the various styles and techniques of bonsai. In Japan training with wire is generally preferred to cutting, the relation of the plant to the container is extremely important and the profile must be asymmetric. Knots, twists and sagging bows are encouraged to give the appearance of antiquity and endurance. A living plant is shaped to enhance the spiritual contemplation of the human mind and express human virtues.

        *   *   *

In all the 'nature-loving' arts the emphasis is on the importance of mastering theory and technique and on a long training and the sheer mental strength needed to obtain the correct mood. It is the same with the chef who makes *sushi* (preparations of raw fish on a bed of rice), those who make lacquerware, origami, pottery, kites and even those who practise the martial arts or calligraphy. I was amazed by the Shinto priest who told me he was exhausted after taking a minute to produce a few characters with the stroke of a brush. The Japanese apply their attributes of discipline and design to modern arts with marvellous results.

Japanese wildlife photographers are among the best in the world and some of them created *Anima*, a natural history magazine which has done much to promote an appreciation of wildlife. Nature photographers like Shinzo Maeda are still defining, selecting and composing. His work follows the seasons and he is fascinated by the everyday, by the design created by frost on leaves or logs stacked against a wall. Some photographers spend a lifetime photographing one species: Mamoru Odajima the brown bear, Tadashi Shimada the kingfisher and

Tsueno Hayashida who has a collection of 35,000 pictures of the crane and its habitat. Some, who have been photographing one subject for more than twenty years, refuse to have them published because they are not yet perfect enough. Whereas westerners generally seek out big close-ups, the Japanese are not afraid to publish a picture where the animal or bird is a speck in a vast landscape.

Nature photography is taking off as a new sport or art. Fujisan has its own band of photographers. One joins the club to learn where to find the shot of cherry blossom that frames the snow-capped peak, or Fujisan reflected in the lake, a red *torii* to one side. In Nikko there is a certain birch tree which thousands of photographers visit each year to catch its autumn splendour glowing through a dawn mist. These photographers repeatedly capture the symbolism of nature just as the early artists copied their masters.

In the 'nature-loving' Japanese arts there are many parallel themes. Nature is extensively contemplated and used to provide subjective inspiration and express human emotions. The expression is distanced from reality and in the final composition, design or effect is more important. If European art is said to dominate nature then Japanese art takes from it. There is nothing

Brown bears in the forests of Hokkaido. Traditionally wild animals and even man were considered to be simply part of the natural world. Japanese photographers are not afraid to publish a picture where the animal is part of the landscape rather than dominating the foreground.

Like sculptural forms shrouded in mist, these whooper swans are less important than the mysterious and wintry atmosphere of the picture.

wrong with taking spiritual inspiration from nature. All cultures do and those who do so to a lesser extent are the poorer for it. But loving or using nature is not the same as understanding her. In fact subjectivity is generally not good ground for the rationality needed to understand nature. Emotions may demand conservation but objectivity is needed to put it into practice. The attitude is typified by Kiyoaki, the hero of Yukio Mishima's *Spring Snow*, whose 'elegance was the thorn . . . a plant without roots' and for whom 'the only thing valid . . . was to live for the emotions – gracious and unstable, dying only to quicken again.' It would be too painful for Kiyoaki to turn his refined mind to the problem of scientific thinking.

Many artists are at the forefront of the grassroots conservation movement but the emotional love of nature evident in Japanese art, against which traditional western art is dry by comparison, should not automatically be used to suggest harmony with nature as it so often is. The Japanese arts have much to teach the world about the spiritual pleasure and inspiration that can be gleaned from nature. But there is no paradox between the strength of nature in the Japanese arts and the country's poor reputation for looking after the wild. Man at one with nature moulds it at his will. The falling petals of full-blown cherry blossoms, likened by a poet to tears shed by a saddened sky, are a reminder that Japan's beauty is fragile.

THE BIRD OF HAPPINESS

Beneath each green pine tree,
Staring at the grains of sand
With such intensity,
What can you so yearn to find?
Cranes, you've soulmates of your kind!

Written by a noblewoman in the tenth century
and translated by Dorothy Britton

Of the many creatures the Japanese have taken from the wild and made into symbols the red-crowned or Japanese crane is their favourite. Village names, poetry and paintings suggest that red-crowned cranes (*Grus japonensis*) once visited many of the Japanese islands. Yet, at the turn of this century it was thought to be extinct in Japan; the symbol appeared to have outlived the real bird. Fortunately a tiny population remained hidden in a vast peat marsh in Hokkaido. The people had been given a second chance.

Today nearly four hundred, more than a third of the world's population of red-crowned cranes, live and breed in Hokkaido. Each crane stays with its partner for life. Early in the year they begin their courtship dancing on the wintering grounds, re-establishing the strong bond which keeps the couple together through the trials of rearing their young. The cranes bob their heads, bow, circle each other and leap high into the air. The urge to dance appears spontaneous and infectious; inspired by one pair, other couples join in.

The cranes' breeding grounds, the marshes along the southeast coast of Hokkaido 30 or so km away, are locked in the grip of ice and snow throughout the winter. In March the pairs return to their previous nesting sites where, if conditions are still suitable, they claim their territories. There is competition for the best sites so the cranes return early while the snow is still adrift

Previous page: *Japanese cranes in the bleak Hokkaido landscape; this pair will remain faithful for life.*

'Fuji from Umesawa' from 'Thirty-six views of Mount Fuji' by Katsushika Hokusai (1760–1849). Mixed flocks of cranes, including red-crowned cranes, depicted near Fujisan support the belief that red-crowned cranes used to winter in the southwest of Japan. (By courtesy of the Board of Trustees of the Victoria & Albert Museum).

When a crane pair starts dancing it is infectious. In the excitement a young crane, identified by its brown head, dances with a crow or a piece of paper for want of a partner.

on the reeds. In a year of heavy snow they will wait for the floodwaters, caused by the snow-melt, to recede. Timing is important for the chicks' survival: if they wait too long, they miss the spring flush of food; and a hard winter, arriving while they are still small and vulnerable, may kill off those which have survived a capricious summer. The cranes choose an area of from 1 to 7 sq km of reed which is often bounded by a stream, trees or hills. The boundary may help in the distinction of territories or make the cranes feel more secure. Feeding areas of

In the past many Japanese cranes flew south ahead of the snow to winter in warmer parts of Japan. Today they stay in Hokkaido throughout the bitter winter, making them all the more special to the local people.

open water are needed within easy flying distance of the nest, but no one knows exactly what makes an ideal breeding marsh.

Both partners build the nest, a platform about a metre across, of reeds and sedge. Spring comes last to eastern Hokkaido. Around Kushiro marsh the cherry trees do not flower until late May and normally by this time the female has laid two eggs. The male shares the thirty-two-day incubation period, changing places with the female about four times a day. The departing bird walks through the reeds, so as not to reveal the location of the nest, before flying off to feed. Periodically the incubating bird turns the eggs with its beak to spread the warmth evenly. Crows, foxes and feral mink are all egg thieves. The canny carrion crows work in pairs. While one distracts the crane off the nest, the other nips in and steals the eggs, smashing and eating them on the spot. Floodwater or reed fires may also threaten the nest. If the cranes lose their first clutch they may lay a second or even a third time.

The second chick hatches about two days after the first and shortly afterwards the parents move their young deep into the reeds to hide them from kites, crows, sea-eagles, mammals and snakes. The parents shepherd the well-camouflaged, tawny chicks, feeding them insects, tadpoles, snails and small fish, while they themselves eat eels, frogs, carp, and the young of other nesting birds such as warbler chicks or ducklings. Each evening the parents make a roosting platform in the reeds. In summer the streams and rivers, flanked by poplars and alder, flow peaty brown, weaving channels through the bright green of the new reed growth. By late summer the chicks are mimicking the adults and learning to deal with the wings of dragonflies or the spines of fish.

The weather is still a hazard; heavy summer rains may last for days, a bitterly cold fog often spreads, smoke-like, through the

A crane pair shepherds its chick to an open pool to forage. At this early age chicks are extremely vulnerable and away from the sanctuary of the tall reeds the parents need to keep a constant watch.

marshes and the hot sun can overheat the chicks. Japanese cranes are, however, renowned for being excellent and attentive parents and they may shield the chicks from both rain and sun with outstretched wings. If it is too hot they sometimes cache their young while they forage in the open pools. As the hot summer dries the pools and the purple irises and yellow day-lilies fade, the cranes' larder disappears. The reeds flower and seed and in early September, as the migrating songbirds pass through on their way south, the crane families move out to the surrounding countryside in search of food. The young learn to tackle new foods as they follow their parents, foraging in the woodland edges and fields for mice, insects and worms. They take bulbs and seeds and are also attracted by corn left in the fields after harvest time. It is there, away from the sanctuary of the marsh, that they come into contact with people.

In ancient times when Japan was the 'Land of the Luxuriant Reed Plains' there was plenty of marshland in the northern parts of the archipelago where the cranes could build their nests. Well camouflaged, and set deep into the marshbeds, they would have been difficult to reach even by canoe. With the onset of winter the cranes probably flew south of what is now Tokyo, to parts of Honshu and Kyushu where snow rarely falls and where they would have been vulnerable to hunters. Folk tales and drawings of wounded cranes suggest that some peasants considered them a good meal.

To the Ainu the crane was the god of the marsh creatures. Today, in areas no longer inhabited by cranes, the Ainu still celebrate the crane in dance. In Biratori, in southwest Hokkaido, seventeen women group together in the shape of a flying crane. Around Lake Akan two women dance around two young girls, raising their kimono skirts to mimic the parent cranes defending their young from bears and birds of prey. Other women accompany them, clapping, stamping and crying in a faithful rendition of an agitated crane. As the dance ends all four fold their wings and curtsey to the ground. The dancemaster explained that only women dance the steps of the crane because only they can attempt to portray the grace and beauty of the bird.

Shinto was inspired to worship beauty and it stressed the importance of cleanliness and purity. So the early Japanese could not fail to have been impressed by the dignified beauty, the pride, grace and nobility of the red-crowned crane. They called the bird *tancho*, meaning red crown, and it became a sacred creature. Many cultures seem to have legends of heroes who turn into great white birds and fly away. Japan has swans, ibis, storks and egrets to choose from but the legendary white

Ainu women dance the steps of the crane dance on the shores of Lake Akan, mimicking the cranes and weaving a charm to keep bears and other frightening creatures away.

bird is almost always the crane. The mythical compilations of the creation of Japan speak of Yamatotakeru-no-Mikoto, a legendary warrior who conquered foes to extend the borders of ancient Japan. On his death his soul took the form of a crane and flew away.

The white cranes with their mournful and echoing cries seemed kindred spirits to the Japanese who have always found pleasure and refinement in melancholy reflection. Cranes, renowned for their fidelity because they pair for life, became metaphors for the wistful yearning of a lost loved one. In the Nara period the poet Tajihi wrote after the death of his wife:

> *The cranes keep calling*
> *Calling as they fly across*
> *Toward the reeds*
> *And oh! so forlorn am I*
> *Who sleep alone tonight.*

'The grateful crane' is one of the oldest and most evocative tales:

A lonely woodcutter chances on a wounded crane. He withdraws an arrow, tends the wound and the crane is able to fly away. Shortly afterwards a beautiful young woman arrives at the woodcutter's cottage. He gives her shelter and in return she promises to weave for him, provided he never watches her at work. The woodcutter receives so much money for the silken white cloth

Facing page: With its grace, purity and nobility it is not difficult to see why the Japanese crane has played such an important role in Japanese culture.

120

that he cannot contain his curiosity. He peeps through the window as she works through the night. Through falling snow he sees the crane as she works at the loom, plucking a last feather from her breast. In the morning the woman, now thin and weak, hands over another bolt of cloth. When she realizes her secret has been discovered, she cries a long mournful adieu. The woodcutter will never be able to look on her again. She turns into a crane and flies away for ever. The man is left looking at an empty blue sky.

The status of the crane increased when, with the arrival of Buddhism in the sixth and seventh centuries, many cultural influences were absorbed from China. In ancient Chinese philosophy the crane was a holy bird, said to be the messenger of legendary sages whom it carried on its back between the various heavenly worlds. The crane, the principal of the celestial world, was adopted as a symbol of longevity as is manifest in the arts of eighth-century Japan.

Cranes were often paired with pine trees – also symbols of long life. Hundreds of examples remain from over the centuries on tea bowls, kimonos, scrolls, hair combs and paintings. In some paintings the white bird is so stylized that it is difficult to be sure whether it is a crane, stork, ibis or an egret. Unlike cranes, these other birds commonly roost in pines. Perhaps the early artists got the birds confused, but it is more likely that the incongruity did not worry them as it was more important that both pine and crane were matched in the world of symbols. Bamboo and turtles were often coupled with pines and cranes, all united by the common longevity theme. ·

Cranes were accorded reverence by Japanese rulers as well as by artists. At Kamakura in the eleventh century Yoshiiye, one of the feudal leaders challenging the power of the emperor, celebrated Hōjōe, the Buddhist festival in which birds and animals are released to set them on the road to freedom. According to legend, in thanksgiving after a successful battle he released hundreds of cranes into the sky. Each had a prayer strip tied to its leg to pray for those killed in the fighting. Another legend speaks of Yoritomo, famed for establishing the Kamakura shogunate, who, a century later, held a similar passion for cranes. His favourite pastime was to attach labels to the legs of white cranes and release them. Those who saw the birds were encouraged to report the fact. Should they capture the cranes, they were asked to write the site on the label and release them again. This is one of the earliest records of an attempt to discover the movements of a bird by marking it in a recognizable way. It is claimed that some of Yoritomo's cranes were sighted several

Facing page: This elegant colour woodcut by Koriusai (c. 1766–88) shows a courtesan paired with stylized representations of a crane, pine and tortoise. Although such an association would be impossible in the natural world, all three were commonly depicted together as symbols of longevity. (By courtesy of the Board of Trustees of the Victoria & Albert Museum)

centuries after his death. Wild cranes are, in fact, thought to live for only forty or fifty years, but the story pays homage to a belief that the crane lived for a thousand years.

Yoshiiye is said to have declared that anyone killing a red-crowned crane would face death. During the age of the shoguns the sacred *tancho* was protected by warlords and samurai. One New Year the ruling shogun presented a *tancho* to the emperor for a banquet. The custom of eating crane meat on special occasions spread among the samurai. As the *tancho* was protected, they flew their goshawks at the other crane species which migrated to Japan in the winter months, the hooded and white-naped cranes. These species were also officially protected from farmers and game hunters but they never attained the special status of the red-crowned crane.

During this period it became popular to dedicate gifts depicting the crane and the turtle to temples and shrines. The crane, promising long life, also came to symbolize health. By the tomb of the shogun Tokugawa Ieyasu (1542–1616) at Nikko a bronze crane stands on top of a turtle. An unlikely association in the natural world, the meaning was, none the less, clear to the seventeenth-century pilgrims who came to pay their respects.

Fidelity, long life, and good health – over the years the crane has become the perfect symbol of good fortune and happiness. The first example of the thousand cranes' motif is generally attributed to the artist Sotatsu who embodied the theme on a 15-m scroll in the early seventeenth century. It was repeated

For Buddhists religious merit could be gained by releasing animals and birds. Seated at Kamakura, with Fujisan in the background, the feudal leader presides over the release of hundreds of cranes, each representing a soldier killed in battle. (Private collection)

Facing page: Crane and turtle by the shogun's tomb at Toshogu Shrine, Nikko. Cranes, believed to live for a thousand years, were often depicted together with tortoises or turtles which were said to live for ten thousand years. In China a mythological beast, a combination of a dragon and a turtle, guards 'the waters' – hence the turtle's dragon-like appearance.

This Japanese fan design (Tosa school) of cranes flying over the waves is a typical example of flying red-crowned cranes being erroneously depicted by artists with completely white wings and black tails. (By courtesy of the Board of Trustees of the Victoria & Albert Museum)

again and again in this and the following century on sliding doors, screens, and lacquerware as well as in literature. While a few leading artists may have travelled to watch wild cranes and others kept a crane in captivity to study, many of the city craftsmen simply copied this popular theme. Mistakes were, therefore, continually repeated. One of the commonest misconceptions was to show the red-crowned cranes with white wings and black tails. In fact only the edge of the crane's wing is etched in black, although when the cranes roost (or stand in captivity) their wings are folded and the long black feathers droop, giving the impression that their tails are black. The crane symbol had become more important than the wild bird.

During the age of the shoguns the crane was protected. But 1868, the year when Emperor Meiji moved the imperial capital to Edo (the home of the last shogunate) and renamed it Tokyo, heralded their downfall. Embracing the ways of the West, the emperor looked to European aristocrats as models for his court. Some Japanese blamed the vegetarian diet for their lack of stature and meat began to appear at banquets. A typical menu included turtle or mutton soup, followed by venison, roast beef, gamecock and quail. Westerners travelling to Japan taught that game shooting like falconry was the accepted sport of the aristocracy. As guns became readily available merchant families and even farmers were keen to taste the meat which had once been reserved for their rulers. Over the twenty years which

Facing page: Kinya Nakajima of the Japan Falconiformes Centre wears the costume of the shogun's personal falconer in the Tokugawa era (Edo period). He carries a goshawk, the falconers' favourite bird, on his wrist. The shoguns gave their protection to the red-crowned cranes, allowing only one to be caught each year by a goshawk for the emperor's New Year feast.

followed the cranes fell victim to this new hunting craze as they foraged round farms in autumn and winter. Nobody issued a new edict to protect their favourite symbol and by the turn of the century the Japanese believed their *tancho* to be extinct.

The crane was not the only large white bird persecuted at the end of the nineteenth century. The Japanese crested ibis (*Nipponia nippon*) foraged in the wet rice paddies for snails, frogs, freshwater crabs and other small water-loving creatures. The farmers blamed it for trampling the rice seedlings, though in all probability it was helping them by taking the insects and snails which were damaging their crop. Although the ibis occasionally featured in art, it never attained the symbolic

The shogun's falconers prepare to catch one red-crowned crane. The protected cranes were accustomed to seeing farmers in the fields, so the cunning falconers dressed as peasants and kept the goshawk out of sight. Ink on paper by Doiku Kawanabe (mid Edo period). (Courtesy of Kinya Nakajima)

'Sweet flags and snowy heron' by Ando Hiroshige (1797–1858). Little egrets, like all white birds, were symbolic of purity. Each prefecture has adopted both a bird and a flower as its symbol: the little egret represents Tokushima. (By courtesy of the Board of Trustees of the Victoria & Albert Museum)

power of the crane and had not been granted protection by the shoguns. Its delicate, pink-tinged feathers were much sought after. They traditionally decorated the most important sword at the shrine of the sun goddess and were also made into dusters for the tea ceremony and the small Buddhist altars at home. After the Meiji restoration the woodland-breeding ibis was systematically shot by farmers, becoming locally extinct over the next ten years in Kyushu, Hokkaido and most of Honshu. In 1893 a law was passed to protect the remaining few but it came too late and by the 1920s the Japanese thought they had lost their ibis as well as their crane. In fact two small groups survived, one on the remote Noto peninsula, the other on off-lying Sado Island.

In the 1950s and 1960s another western scourge drastically affected Japanese wildlife: pesticides were introduced to improve agricultural efficiency. Rice fields were a prime target and the ibis was especially vulnerable. Pesticides were blamed for the infertility of eggs. Few young were born and numbers dropped again, leaving a population of only ten birds in the 1960s. The last few ibis were brought into captivity in the hope that they would breed. The project failed and now only four (including one donated from China) remain in captivity in Japan and there are only twenty-one known individuals left in the world.

The oriental white stork (*Ciconia boyciana*) has a similar history. A tree nester like the ibis, it bred over much of Honshu but by the turn of the century only one small colony remained at the top of a hill in southwest Honshu. Like the ibis, the storks fed from rice paddies and became contaminated with pesticides. The last three young fledged successfully in 1959 and the last breeding bird died in 1971. The white stork has not bred since in Japan.

The symbolic status of birds like egrets, mandarin ducks and the ptarmigan did nothing to protect them from the hunters' guns. The grouse-like rock ptarmigan (*Lagopus mutus*) lives in the alps of central Japan. In the summer its mottled grey-brown plumage blends with the rocky mountain escarpments and in winter its white coat is beautifully camouflaged against the snow. The ptarmigan, because it lived safely through the thunder and lightning emanating from the mountains, was known as the thunder bird. It was thought to protect people from the ravages of storms and many mountain huts have a ptarmigan carved over their doors. But the ground-living, docile bird was easy prey for hunters and became locally extinct on a number of mountain ranges.

The short-tailed albatross (*Diomedea albatrus*), which breeds

*The rare short-tailed albatross
breeds in colonies only on
Torishima and the Senkaku Islands.
One of about twenty bird species
endemic to Japan, it was once
thought to be extinct but, after
strict protection, its total numbers
stand at approximately 350.*

only in Japan, used to nest in thousands on Torishima, a small volcanic island some 600 km south of Tokyo. The albatross spends the summer at sea, returning in October to Torishima to nest on the ground in a vast colony. In 1886 a group of people settled on the island to make a living gathering feathers to stuff *futon* or quilts. Soon three hundred down hunters were working the tiny 6-km island and within fifteen years over five million albatrosses had been killed. Then, in 1902, the island erupted, killing the inhabitants and ruining part of the albatrosses' breeding area. The remaining birds had a few years' respite but in the 1930s the profitable down industry reopened the slaughter. In August 1939 Torishima erupted again and the short-tailed albatross was believed to be extinct. A few ocean-wandering birds survived, however, and in 1950 ten birds were discovered. Hunting was prohibited on the island and today, after strict protection, the colony is 250 strong.

The copper pheasant (also endemic to Japan), golden and sea-eagles, otters, wolves, sika deer, the serow and brown and black bears were all popular targets for the sportsmen. Gradually, as it became increasingly difficult for the aristocrats to find their game, they realized that wildlife was disappearing at an alarming rate. In 1892 twenty-four years after the Meiji government had come to power, it issued game laws controlling the use of guns. Protection of some species, such as the oriental white stork and the ptarmigan, followed. Unfortunately these measures came too late for the wolf and other creatures such as the stork and otter whose dwindling populations were hit by pesticides in the 1950s. The last body of a wild Japanese otter (*Lutra lutra whiteleyi*) was found in 1983, although possible otter tracks have been sighted since.

In this short space of time the Japanese had lost much of their wildlife. The red-crowned crane gave them a reprieve. In 1924 a hunter reported seeing some cranes in Kushiro marsh in south-east Hokkaido. Although the Japanese crane had been strictly protected by the shoguns, their control did not extend to Hokkaido. A record dating from the late seventeenth century states that two cranes were offered as gifts by the Ainu to the encroaching Japanese and records from the following century show that salted crane meat was exported to the mainland. None the less the crane population held its own in Hokkaido's large southern coastal marshes. After the restoration in 1868 the Japanese flocked to Hokkaido in earnest and many more cranes were killed. They also lost their breeding habitat as the pioneers reclaimed huge areas of marshland for cultivation. By the turn of the century ornithologists in Tokyo believed the bird to be extinct. Dr Masatomi, a crane biologist, believes that Kushiro marsh was saved from reclamation because it was too cold to grow rice. In 1924 six nests were found and the total population was estimated to be less than twenty birds. In 1925 hunting was prohibited over 1,200 hectares of the marsh. By 1934 the cranes numbered about thirty, and the following year the crane was declared a natural monument. Natural monument status was one of the early conservation measures in Japan. The choice of the word 'monument' was an extension of a title already conferred on great temples and works of art.

Natural monument status protected a creature from being killed outright but it did not take account of its food requirements, nor did it protect its habitat. So, despite their protected status, the total number of red-crowned cranes remained at around thirty, still a dangerously low number. In the particularly harsh winter of 1950 heavy snow blanketed the Kushiro area. The wary cranes were driven to forage close to farms, picking at grains from cobs and drying straw in the recently harvested fields. One farmer, Mr Yamazaki threw out some corn to the cranes. Two years later schoolchildren from Tsuruimura village saw the hungry cranes on their way home and decided to feed them. They asked their parents for money to buy grain from

Cranes roost overnight in rivers which, fed by volcanic hot springs, continue to flow despite the freezing temperatures and, away from the bank, the slumbering cranes are also safer from wild dogs and foxes.

farmers and they scattered the corn in the snow. Gradually the cranes overcame their caution and thirty-three birds came regularly to feed. National interest was fired and money was donated to buy more food. The following winter was warmer but, to the delight of the children, the cranes returned. They had remembered their feeding ground and brought nine newcomers. Tsuruimura (which means 'village where cranes come') was firmly on the map. The cranes were also fed regularly at Tanchnosato (meaning 'home of the crane') and in the early 1960s other farmers like Mr Ito and Mrs Watanabe began feeding the cranes – as they still do today. The effect on the crane population was spectacular as the initial steep rise in the graph on page 132 shows. By 1962 there were 184 wintering cranes. (The local people eagerly awaited the return of their birds. Some even took the train past Kayanuma station, where the cranes were also fed, to catch the first winter sighting.) Thus it was farmers and their children who forged the first new link between the people and the wild crane.

During the 1960s, however, the spectacular increase in the crane population slowed down. In some years the counts on the

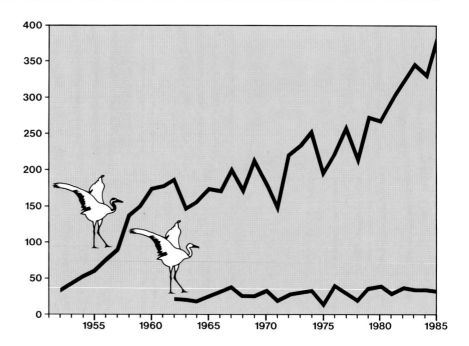

Population trends of adult and young red-crowned cranes in Hokkaido: the upper line of the graph shows the total population, the lower line the number of young counted on or around 5 December at the cranes' winter feeding grounds. (Figures courtesy of the Environment Agency)

winter feeding grounds showed that numbers had actually fallen by twenty or more. The main cause of death was collision with electricity wires as the cranes flew in. In the 1970s the Hokkaido Electric Power Company began to put yellow plastic markers over the wires on the main flyway of the cranes. Nowadays only a few young birds are killed this way. Numbers began to increase again during the 1970s and, as the population (which started growing in the 1950s) is relatively young, few birds are dying of old age.

Yet the frightening fact is that, although the adult population is steadily increasing, the winter counts clearly show that the cranes are not raising more young. The population is producing roughly the same number of chicks as it did when it was only half the size. In 1985 101 pairs attempted to breed but on the winter feeding grounds there were only thirty-two young in a population of 384 birds. The chicks cannot be accurately counted until they reach the wintering grounds as juveniles and no one is yet sure why their numbers are so low. The cause may be lack of suitable breeding sites, failure of the eggs to hatch, high mortality among the chicks or a combination of all three.

When the cranes first began to increase they spread east of Kushiro to nest in the marshes scattered along the coast. Yet while their numbers have grown, these marshes have been rapidly disappearing. Many are owned by small farmers and as government subsidies have become available the land has been drained for growing crops or grazing livestock. Large marshes such as Kushiro have been further affected by the encroachment of industry and forestry. Real estate is big business and Kushiro, with its profitable paper mills and expanding port, sees the marsh as wasted land. Drainage takes water from the nearest marshland; as it dries it is colonized by scrubby vegetation, giving the developers an excuse to take a bit more. Many of the surrounding hills have been denuded of their deciduous vegetation. This prevents them from retaining water and regulating its flow into the marsh. Heavy rains flush away large amounts of loose earth which dam up the marsh, accelerating the drying-out process. The histories of individual marshes, which have lost their breeding pairs, are well charted but it is much more difficult to get a picture of the whole vast area. Disturbance is often cited as a stress factor yet cranes have successfully reared chicks a few kilometres from villages without the people even knowing they were there.

In 1967 the small protected area within the 29,000 hectares of Kushiro marsh was enlarged to about 5,000 hectares but in the early 1970s scientists pointed out that this area was only large enough for about eight pairs. In 1980 the protected area was declared a Ramsar site, an international status which ranks it among the best wetlands in the world. Despite this, the actual protection is only as good as the country makes it. In 1983 the Wild Bird Society of Japan published a paper stating that of twenty-four breeding areas only three had 'not yet been adversely influenced by development' while 'eight areas will certainly become unsuitable as nesting sites in the near future'. As Dr Fujimaki, a crane biologist, says, 'Industry is still winning.'

The failure of eggs to hatch is an equally worrying factor.

Hokkaido, with its vast, open plains, has become the grain and dairy belt of Japan. Huge areas of marshland, once breeding grounds for cranes, have been reclaimed for agriculture and many surrounding hills have lost their forest cover – extremely important for regulating and maintaining the essential flow of water into the reedbeds.

Nobody is sure of the cause. Some eggs are deserted because of natural hazards but in many cases the female sits on an egg long after it was due to hatch before eventually abandoning it. Some eggs are infertile and never start to grow, others die at a later stage. If the scientists are able to retrieve these eggs before the predators they can assess the stage of development that the egg has reached. Data collected intermittently in the early research years suggested that about 20 per cent of the eggs which were normally incubated failed to hatch. But some scientists think the situation may be far worse. It is a frightening and little-understood phenomenon which they are just beginning to investigate. Research from other bird populations suggests that pesticides washed into the marsh waterways may be a likely cause. Or it could be the result of inbreeding, a tragic legacy from the days when there were only twenty red-crowned cranes left in Hokkaido.

The chicks are at their most vulnerable in the first three months of life when mortality in the wild is estimated to be as high as 50 per cent. Conservationists agree that the major scientific work should concentrate on the breeding sites, but fear of disturbance has made it difficult to get permission for this and kept research to a minimum.

It is not much easier to carry out research on the wintering grounds. Ringing is a scientifically accepted method of gathering basic information on bird movements, migration patterns and longevity. But local people worry that catching and ringing the cranes will frighten them away for good. It was only last year that scientists finally obtained permission to bait and ring some cranes, provided it was done away from the traditional feeding sites. Unfortunately there was plenty of food elsewhere and the cranes were not interested. However, 1,300 km south of Kushiro at Izumi on Kyushu Island scientists have been ringing the migrant hooded crane (*Grus monacha*) and white-naped crane (*Grus vipio*) on their wintering grounds since 1982. The hooded cranes leave their Siberian breeding grounds and the white-naped cranes Mongolia, Manchuria and southern Siberia in the autumn, arriving at Kyushu in October.

Kyushu and southwestern Honshu have been traditional wintering grounds over many centuries for thousands of hooded and white-naped cranes. Shooting and the gradual reclamation of the southern wetlands caused the demise of the visiting cranes. Some held out in the Izumi area of Kagoshima because this coastal wetland was protected from the mainland by rivers. But during the Second World War the cranes were heavily shot by hungry people and soon after Izumi was also drained. By

1945 the hooded crane population was down to 250, and the white-naped to twenty-five birds until Mr Matano, a local farmer, began to feed them.

Today about seventy hooded cranes winter at Yashiro in Yamaguchi prefecture in southern Honshu. Another six thousand congregate in Izumi and, apart from occasional reports of small groups in Korea and other parts of Japan, these account for the total world population. They are joined by over a thousand white-naped cranes, about a third of the total known world population, and occasionally by vagrants from other species who, through some mishap, have become caught in the wrong flyway. Recent records include the demoiselle, sandhill, common and Siberian white cranes. This huge gathering of cranes is one of the ornithological wonders of Japan. In 1953 the white-naped crane was designated a 'special natural monument' and 51 hectares of paddy field were leased from the farmers by the Cultural Agency. The rice crop left behind short stubble creating an ideal place for the cranes to be fed each winter.

As the crane numbers have increased, the birds have spread locally to look for food and have been accused of eating potatoes, Chinese cabbage, wheat and broad beans and of trampling down the raised banks between the rice paddies. The farmers

The six thousand or so hooded cranes which winter in Izumi near Kagoshima account for almost the entire world population. Joined by about a thousand white-naped cranes and vagrants from other crane species, they are fed in a small protected area but overcrowding has forced some of them into the surrounding farmland.

have tried to protect their crops with plastic bubbles and streamers but this is expensive and not always effective. Farmers who have cranes regularly feeding on their land outside the 51 hectares believe that they too should be entitled to rent.

The Wild Bird Society of Japan is also monitoring the situation at Izumi. They are worried that almost the entire population of one crane species is concentrated into such a small, overcrowded area and plan to research the possibility of finding other sites where the cranes might winter safely.

In 1985 the Wild Bird Society began a national fund-raising 'Crane Campaign'. Its aim is to raise money for the wild bird by reawakening the close affinity of the Japanese people with the crane symbol. Both the cranes and the people need land but the agricultural and construction lobbies are richer and more powerful than the conservation groups. The crane does, however, have one advantage in Japan; although the wild bird nearly became extinct, the strength of its symbol did not diminish. During the Meiji period when the arts were influenced by contemporary western styles, artists continued to paint favourite subjects like the crane. In the 1950s and 1960s a number of prominent businesses adopted the crane as a logo. Japan Air Lines did so in 1965, saying that the crane, a bird which in folklore stood for longevity and good luck, was highly appropriate. A number of liquor manufacturers promote sake using crane designs similiar to ancient family crests.

The promise of fidelity, long life, good fortune and happiness made the crane the perfect symbol of marriage and today the wedding industry remains loyal to the crane symbol. Red and white are the colours of happy occasions and cranes traditionally adorned the bride's wedding kimono, just as decorations in the shape of cranes were exchanged by bride and groom when their engagement was announced.

Today, weddings are a growth industry. A wedding company will provide everything a couple needs including the religious ceremony and offer a choice of banquet menus, gifts for the guests, kimonos, hairstyles and honeymoons. Menu cards, gifts and wrapping paper are decorated with cranes; sweet cakes are baked in the shape of cranes and at one wedding banquet a huge ice carving of a crane and chick stood by the side of the top table. In the subways and at railway stations cranes are depicted on wedding company adverts. As wedding companies heartily exploit the crane symbol conservationists suggested that they might donate some money to the Crane Campaign. Today wedding guests at the Tamahimeden wedding hall are politely shown the Wild Bird Society campaign display and a collection

Wedding kimonos are traditionally decorated with cranes. This young couple was the first to donate money to the Wild Bird Society's 'Crane Campaign' during their wedding ceremony.

box. Artists have also supported the campaign by sketching pictures of the crane for auction and the society has taken newspaper space to advertise it, raising £120,000 in the first two years.

But the Crane Campaign is in its early days and has only earned a fraction of the potential donations and sponsorship. Also, the society has many more other birds to worry about. It is, for example, waging a campaign against the poaching of wild birds for *yakitori* or 'grilled bird'. The birds are caught by stringing mist nets between bushes – nets so fine that birds fly

Yakitori or grilled bird. The Japanese invented mist nets, originally made of silk, for catching wild birds to eat. Today this is illegal and the Wild Bird Society is compaigning against poachers who, with birds selling from £1.50 to £4.00 each, can make as much as £2,000 in a season.

Few people have caught a glimpse of the newly discovered Okinawa rail in the wild but tourists visiting the region are constantly greeted by its symbol.

straight into them. Sparrows, dusky thrushes and visiting song-birds were traditional *yakitori* fare. Today *yakitori* bars serve skewered chicken, and catching wild birds to eat, stuff or keep as pets is illegal. *Yakitori* was, however, originally a rural dish and the Wild Bird Society believes that around four million songbirds may be poached each year. Bullheaded shrikes, bul-buls, oriental greenfinches, sparrowhawks and rarities like the collared scops owl have all died in *yakitori* nets.

Some society members have masqueraded as poachers in Gifu prefecture in order to pass on information to the police, and in Tochigi prefecture a local group has also organized watchers around the clock at goshawk eyries to deter poachers from stealing the young. A young goshawk could sell for as much as £1,800 and a stuffed adult can cost up to £400.

The society also hopes to influence the protection of the unique Okinawa rail (*Rallus okinawae*), a bird known to the locals but only discovered and described by ornithologists as recently as 1981. The Okinawa rail is a distinctive member of the rail family with a large bright red bill, red legs and feet. It lives and feeds in dense swampy forest. The rail is flightless; it climbs trees and floats, fluttering its weak wings, down to the ground. If threatened, it escapes by running extremely fast. Few people see the rail in the wild, yet tourists who visit Okinawa cannot escape its image. At the airport sake bottles, cakes, cigarette packets and pottery are adorned with its symbol. A 'speedy printing' firm has taken the rail as its logo; in the main fishmarket rails are incorporated into the tile design on the floor and a number of buses have a painted rail running along their sides.

Early surveys estimated a total of only twenty or thirty birds but research work by Mark Brazil and Hiroshi Ikenaga suggested that the population was considerably higher. By playing back taped recordings to stimulate calling they received more than 150 responses from individual rails. In 1985 a Wild Bird Society count estimated that there were between 1,500 and 2,000 birds.

Okinawa is the largest of the semi-tropical Ryukyu Islands. Far away from Tokyo, they escaped much of the industry that affected the other main islands in the archipelago. Now these islands are a development zone and money is being poured in with seemingly little thought for local traditions and natural resources. The islands are home to four more endemic species of birds: the Amami woodcock, Lidth's jay, the Ryukyu robin and Pryer's woodpecker. A handsome brown- and chestnut-streaked bird, the woodpecker needs mature forest in which to nest, and today only about a hundred are thought to survive in Okinawa.

The woodpecker, like the Okinawa rail and the red-crowned crane, is one of the twelve avian 'special natural monuments'. Yet, despite the fact that the Okinawa rail is a popular local symbol, in recent years huge areas of its forest home have been replaced by pineapple plantations and other development. In many areas of Japan it seems that the lesson of the red-crowned crane still goes unheeded.

The Wild Bird Society has recently spent some of the money raised by the Crane Campaign on buying one of the red-crowned cranes' feeding sites as a sanctuary. The current emphasis on the winter feeding sites has been criticized since the cranes are relatively safe and the government provides the money for plenty of food. Instead, it is argued, the money should be spent on buying some of the small, vulnerable marsh-lands where cranes breed. The Wild Bird Society maintains that because they are outsiders from Tokyo they have to establish themselves in the area first. They hope to attract more of the people who come to the area to see the cranes in winter to their cause. Although birdwatching is a long way from habitat conservation, it is an important starting point. Money to buy the sanctuary was actually raised from a nationwide sponsored birdwatch or birdathon. The Wild Bird Society, which has 17,000 members, is in a good position to influence the political climate and call for the protection of more breeding habitat.

In 1986 conservationists received some positive news, a proposal from the Environment Agency to designate two-thirds of Kushiro marsh a national park. Although national park designation has a tradition of encouraging hotels, souvenir

With its '1,000 islands conservation campaign' the Wild Bird Society hopes to protect some areas of native forest in the Ryukyu Islands from pineapple plantations and other intensive land use.

shops, car parks and other tourist facilities, the move is generally welcomed by naturalists who believe that local support for the crane will keep tourist development on the marsh to a minimum. They also hope that the park will not detract from the importance of the smaller breeding marshes. While development continues, each year fewer cranes will have the chance to breed and the population will be unlikely to increase its range.

Scientists believe that there are other areas further afield where the crane could find nesting and wintering sites. Two pairs from the Japanese population have already moved across to breed in neighbouring islands. Most crane experts believe that while the cranes which migrated south from Hokkaido were shot, the present population survives from a small group which always spent winter in the area. They may have survived the cold winters by feeding in areas where hot volcanic springs kept the water flowing and provided plenty of food.

Today, towards the end of the year, as the ground hardens and the snow falls, the *tancho* move from the woods and fields surrounding the marsh closer to the feeding sites. At night, safe from predators, they roost in the shallows of a river with head and one leg tucked into the body as the temperature plunges. When the bank vegetation is iced in hawfrost and the air temperature below −25°C the river still flows. At dawn, as the low sun gradually warms the frozen air, the length of the river steams like a Japanese bath. The cranes stay put until they consider it warm enough to fly to the feeding grounds.

In February 1986 I watched the cranes roost on a morning when the temperature was below −18°C. The landscape was snow white, etched with stark trees and bisected by a black river. In the water the slumbering cranes looked like rocks on which snow had rested. The orange sun rose, but it was so bitter that my hair gathered hawfrost. The cranes did not stir until midday when the sun was high in the sky. By that time I was waiting for them at the feeding grounds. Their loud echoing bugle warned that they were on their way. They came, wing tips splayed, soaring high against the brilliant blue sky. Gleaming white, they seemed to radiate light as they spiralled down from the sun. It was so cold that they kept their feet tucked under them until the very last minute. I thought they would bellyflop in the snow but suddenly they changed course to avoid the power lines and disappeared behind the pines to fly in along the river.

As they landed their momentum kept them running and their feet sank in the soft snow. They had to balance carefully to keep from floundering. They arrived in ones and twos trumpeting loudly. The pairs walked in unison as though on tiptoe, then

Roosting cranes at dawn near Akan. Scientists think this population survives from a few birds which, despite the sub-zero temperatures, did not migrate but spent the entire winter in this area.

circled, their heads and beaks pointing to the sky, before settling to feed. Then, for no obvious reason, a pair began to dance. Inspired by the leaping, bowing and twirling of their neighbours another pair began to leap up high, then float gently down. Sometimes one would pick up a twig and throw it high into the air. One crane, either with no one to dance with or because he didn't like the intruder, began to prance at a crow. A youngster played with a magazine which he repeatedly tossed up, his feet paddling through the air as he tried to catch it. A fox came to scavenge and a white-tailed eagle watched from above.

At the feeding sites were hundreds of jostling photographers waiting to capture the cranes dancing in the snow. Photographing cranes became a passion of Tsuneo Hayashida (a local doctor) and his evocative pictures reveal the hidden beauty of the cranes to hundreds. Just as artists joined schools and followed a master, so crane photographers have formed clubs and, following Hayashida, made the wild crane their subject. They use an expensive array of the most powerful lenses available and are told where to wait to get 'that shot' of for

Each year thousands of schoolchildren visit Hiroshima Peace Park to lay colourful wreaths of folded paper cranes at the memorial to Sadako Sasaki.

instance 'flying cranes silhouetted against the setting sun'.

The symbol may have lost its link with the wild bird but it does not mean they cannot be re-united. In 1949 the playwright Junji Kinoshita turned the traditional fairytale of 'the grateful crane' into an award-winning play about the struggle between materialistic and spiritual values. Greedy rogues persuade the woodcutter to force his 'crane wife' to weave more and more cloth. At the end, as in the original tale, the crane flies away for ever. The play's message is particularly poignant for it is this same struggle which will ultimately determine the fate of the wild crane. In the spirit of the Japanese love of pathos and nostalgia, if the crane became extinct it would make an excellent symbol of sadness. The cranes could be returned to the artists as martyrs. But there are hundreds of people who are working hard to save the living 'bird of happiness'. They now have a chance to turn the fate of the wild Japanese crane into their first major conservation success. Every December, following the tradition of the children who first fed the cranes, the schoolchildren of southeast Hokkaido visit all the possible wintering sites in a coordinated effort to count the total population.

And each year new schoolchildren arrive to greet the most powerful symbol of the crane which stands at the Peace Park in Hiroshima. Ever since Sotatsu painted his thousand cranes, the Japanese have folded paper cranes and given them as lucky charms to sick people. A twelve-year-old girl, Sadako Sasaki, a victim of the atom bomb, lay gravely ill in hospital. She began to fold a thousand origami cranes and children from all over the country folded cranes in the hope that she might live. She died with thirty-six cranes left to fold. Her memorial is at the Peace Park. She stands, her hands held high, holding a paper crane.

In the Peace Park I watched as hundreds of schoolchildren placed colourful streamers of paper cranes around the memorial. I went round the exhibition in the museum with David, our film director, and when we came out it was raining. Thousands of schoolchildren crowded round and, thinking we were American, indicated with their fingers the V sign which in Japan stands for both victory and peace. One child shyly raised a hand to David, almost 2 m tall. Suddenly thousands of children milled around gazing up, all wanting to shake hands, and in the disturbance hundreds of pigeons took to the air. In my mind that scene is linked with an image of cranes dancing in the snow. The rain and the cherry blossom falling on the children mingles with the snow scattered by the cranes as they twirl and pirouette.

Cranes greet each other or announce their territory with a special 'unison call'. The reverberating trumpet, which can be heard from 3 km away, has led to the expression **tsuru no hitokoe** *(the voice of the crane) meaning an authoritative voice.*

LONG LIFE TO THE SEA

My shell is proof that once I lived:
Had I not lived, there would have been
no shell.

Mushanokoji Saneatsu
Written in the twentieth century and
translated by Dorothy Britton

The 3,900 or so islands which comprise the Japanese archipelago have nearly 32,500 km of coastline and the Japanese have explored and harvested to the full the wealth of life in the surrounding sea. Every little bay has its history and every coastal village its legends. Not far from the shrine of the sun goddess at Ise are the 'wedded rocks' which represent the deities Izanagi and Izanami, the creators of Japan in Shinto legend. They are linked by a braided straw rope, which is ceremonially replaced each New Year. Pilgrimages are made to witness the sun rise through the cleft between the rocks.

Sacred rocks and islands have been named all around Japan's coastline. On a deserted shore one will often find a red *torii* set against the cliffs or a straw rope wrapped around a rock. Each year sea festivals are held in hundreds of fishing villages. In the boat festival at Miyajima the sea goddess is rowed by priests at high tide through the sacred 'floating' *torii*, dramatizing an ancient legend. Some festivals are concerned with safeguarding the fishermen at sea while others invoke the gods to provide a good harvest. Others celebrate the sea as a well of purity which will cleanse the people and their crops of pestilence.

The story of the legendary fisherboy, Urashima Taro, is a favourite with every child. It describes how some children were teasing a sea-turtle which was stranded on its back. Urashima rescued the turtle and it swam out to sea. A few days later a

*The **torii** at the entrance to the Itsukushima shrine in Miyajima.*

Facing page: *'Turtles and waterweeds' by Gakutei c. 1819. Part of the poem reads: 'The aimless movements of the turtles, like a child, bestow the blessings of long life'. (Chester Beatty Library)*

Previous page: *Japan's Pacific coast is rich in sea life: more than twenty species of small cetaceans have been sighted in these waters.*

turtle invited him to ride on its back. Together they journeyed through the magical underwater kingdom to the sea palace. Urashima had a wonderful time. He met the sea goddess and was entertained by the sea creatures. Three hundred or so years later the turtle returned Urashima to his village. In the Tango peninsula in southern Honshu, Urashima Taro is remembered at the Ura shrine where the casket given to him by the sea goddess and an old scroll of the story are kept. The legend, one of the oldest in Japanese folklore, is thought to be based on fact. Ancient records refer to a fisherboy named Urashima from the province of Tango who vanished out to sea in the year 477. His return is recorded in 825 but he then disappeared again. In oriental lore turtles, like tortoises, are symbols of long life, believed to live for ten thousand years. This idea was reinforced by the fronds of algae which attach to the carapaces of freshwater turtles resembling an old man's beard.

The sea-turtle on the beach at Tango would have been a loggerhead. The loggerhead (*Caretta caretta*) is the third largest of seven species of sea-turtles. Its large head accommodates the powerful muscles needed for crunching sea-cucumbers, sea-

'Ki-ki-mio-mio' (very, very droll!). This triptych of turtles is another example of the depiction of animals with human faces (see page 101). (Museum of Fine Arts, Springfield, Massachusetts. The Raymond A. Bidwell Collection)

snails, crabs, mussels and other shellfish which make up its basic diet. The loggerhead is the commonest sea-turtle found in Japan and it normally breeds on the southwestern beaches. The few individually sighted as far north as Sendai on the east coast or Kanazawa on the west are near the edge of their Pacific breeding range. A few green turtles (*Chelonia mydas*) and an occasional hawksbill (*Eretmochelys imbricata*) breed in the Ryukyu Islands and leathery turtles (*Dermochelys coriacea*) and olive ridleys (*Lepidochelys olivacea*) have also been sighted. Loggerheads are seen off the coast by fishermen from March onwards as they arrive to court and mate in the rocky shallows.

Fishermen traditionally have a special relationship with the sea-turtle. Loggerheads generally arrive on the same warm current which brings in the shoals of fish. Their shells, pitted and worn from many years in the sea, are covered with seaweed and barnacles. Ghost shrimps and small fish often travel with the turtles, either grazing on their backs or using their bulk to provide shelter from predators. The turtles which become entangled in fishing nets are seen as lucky omens, divine harbingers of a good catch, and before they are released, fishermen toast them in sake and pour it over them.

Although freshwater turtle meat has long been thought to increase stamina, sea-turtles are not usually hunted and eaten in Japan. It was often pointed out to me that it is the Europeans not the Japanese who are the connoisseurs of turtle meat although a few of Tokyo's exotic food restaurants have recently imported the custom of eating green sea-turtles. In a few villages in

Kagoshima, Wakayama and Kochi prefectures fishermen also now hunt and eat loggerheads, a practice learned while harvesting pearls in northern Australia. It is not a regular fishery; the boats go out to fish and chase any turtles they sight in the short season. The turtles dive as soon as they sense danger, except for those preoccupied with mating which are an easy target. The fishermen throw a harpoon attached to a rope and if it lodges in the turtle it is hauled aboard. Once out of the water it offers little resistance, its open mouth and rasping breath the only sign of its pain. The fishermen usually tie the turtle to the harbour wall or flip it on its back and eat it on the beach, unceremoniously cutting it up and placing it in a pot over the fire.

Those living in remote areas enjoy the turtle hunt, the taste of the meat and the extra money it provides. According to Dr Itaru Uchida, Japan's leading authority on sea-turtles, an estimated 100 to 150 turtles are caught in this way each year, perhaps not enough to have a significant effect on the future of the population, but still one of the many hazards the turtles face as they arrive near the coast to lay their eggs. The wide-ranging loggerhead, while not as heavily exploited as most other sea-turtles, is

The loggerhead, the commonest turtle to visit Japan's shores, is the most wide ranging of the seven sea-turtle species. Its large head accommodates the heavy musculature needed for crunching crabs and other hard-shelled seafood.

nevertheless classified as vulnerable in the Red Data Book of threatened species and the number that visit Japan's shores has rapidly declined since the Second World War.

Sea-turtles are reptiles. Descended from terrestrial creatures, they are constrained by the need to come ashore to lay their eggs. Nobody is sure what makes a good turtle rookery; many stretches of beach lie empty, while others are crowded with nests. From late May the females emerge from the sea at night and haul themselves laboriously over the sand. Well above the high tide mark, they begin to dig, their hind flippers deftly twisting and turning as they scoop the sand from under them. It takes about half an hour to dig a nest 60 cm deep. Then each female begins to lay. More than a hundred glossy ping-pong-ball-like eggs drop into the hole and she flippers the sand back over them. Experiments have shown that the temperature affects the sex of the hatchlings, so the positioning of the nest and amount of sand covering it is crucial. If the eggs become too hot or too cold they will not develop. As the female lays, her tears secrete salt and she appears exhausted but, vulnerable on land, she heads for the sea well before sunrise. Each female returns to the rookery to lay at fortnightly intervals, two or three times a season. Then she disappears, swallowed up by the depths of the ocean, leaving the eggs to develop alone.

Where the sea-turtles go and what they do remains one of the great mysteries of biology. Only females come ashore to lay. Once the males have hatched they rarely touch dry land again.

Hatchlings emerging from the sand. The baby turtles split the soft shell with their egg teeth and enter a small pocket of air. Then, using their flippers to 'paddle', the mass of turtles gradually rises to the surface.

Sea-turtles would be less vulnerable to predators if they could stay at sea. It is the need to lay eggs on land which brings the females ashore. In a few villages loggerheads were taken for food during the Second World War.

Although sea-turtles come to the surface at hourly intervals to breathe, they are hardly ever sighted at sea. They usually travel alone and scientists know far less about their movements than they do about those of whales. Loggerheads are thought to migrate shorter distances than one population of green sea-turtles which travels 3,200 km from its birthplace to feed. Dr Uchida has tried to gain more information by tagging the females while they are on land. By placing temperature- or depth-recording gadgets on their backs and collecting them when the female returns to lay her second clutch, he has discovered that turtles can dive to over 100 m but tend to swim at 20–30 m deep in water between 10° and 15°C. He has also fitted radio transmitters which have been tracked by satellite. The signal is only received when the turtle surfaces and the longest offshore recording was 320 km.

Turtle eggs provide rich eating and for some villagers have always been a welcome extra food source. In season it is possible to buy sea-turtle eggs at the Tokyo fish market and at certain speciality restaurants. In one exotic dish a turtle egg is cracked over a bed of yam and raw fish and then whipped into the dish with chopsticks. In the 1970s the belief in the turtle as a symbol of longevity joined forces with oriental medicine and the new health fad, and in cities like Osaka turtle eggs made into a stamina drink became a popular health tonic. Heavy poaching began on some beaches; and the price of eggs had increased tenfold to £30 per hundred by 1983.

Little is known about turtles at sea. With a team of scientists, Dr Itaru Uchida has been trying to discover more about their movements by attaching recording devices to the females which visit Gamoda beach in Tokushima. These are put in place when the female is preoccupied with egg laying and are removed a fortnight or so later when she returns to lay her second batch.

The eggs are not difficult to find since the female's tracks are clearly visible in the sand. At Fukiage beach in southwest Kyushu, poachers followed the tracks at night on trail motorbikes to locate every single nest. In the early 1980s a student concluded that no hatchlings were reaching the sea and that, if intensive poaching continued, Fukiage would eventually be lost as a nesting site. It was only through the efforts of fellow-students who spent their summer holidays guarding the beach and confronting the poachers that eventually the local government granted Fukiage official protection. Elsewhere, following the initiative of some junior high school children, several schools have run projects associated with protecting or researching sea-turtles. At a few schools on the Pacific coast eggs are taken from one or two nests and placed into crates. The eggs are covered in sand in conditions which mimic the nest as closely as possible but are not heated or regulated in any way. When the eggs hatch the turtles are released immediately. It is thought that the first few hours may be vital for picking up chemical or other signals from the sand or seawater. Scientists have suggested that these may be used by the females years later. When they return to the coastal waters the signals may guide the mature turtles to their natal beach to lay eggs.

After about eight weeks the eggs begin to hatch. The baby turtle splits the soft shell using an 'egg tooth' on its snout and enters a small pocket of air left between the eggs and the sand. Using their flippers in a paddling motion, the mass of turtles climbs to the surface. Their activity slows down when sun warms the sand, a mechanism which ensures that they emerge at night. It may be three or four days after the first turtle has hatched before the last reaches the surface. In a rookery which has not been robbed by predators or wiped out by typhoons about 65 per cent of the eggs hatch.

The hatchlings orientate towards the faint glimmer of light reflected from the sea surface. They are tiny, not much larger than a matchbox, and highly vulnerable. Like water boatmen, their flippers work constantly as they make their way towards the sea. Many get tangled in flotsam. Any left by morning are eaten by kites, crows, feral cats or dogs. Once in the sea they paddle hard to get away from the dangerous coastal waters. Kites and gulls swoop down to pluck them from the sea and dolphin-fish and sharks sneak underneath to grab them.

The egg yolk sustains the hatchlings for about three days, after which, drifting with the currents, probably in seaweed rafts, they feed on small invertebrates or plankton. No one knows exactly where they go or how they find food. Like the adults, they disappear. Dr Uchida has tried to solve the mystery by plotting the sea currents and tagging some of the hatchlings although it is difficult to devise a permanent tag for such a small sea creature. His findings suggest that the hatchlings drift northwards on a current which eventually reaches the west coast of America. But once they have left Japan's coast the puzzle remains. Some sub-adults have been found off the coast of the Philippines, Taiwan and China. At around four years old the sea-turtles can swim hard and dive deeply. But it will be at least fifteen years before they return to their natal waters as mature adults to court and mate.

In addition to hunters and egg thieves, the sea-turtles also face the problem of coastal development. Today there are only six major nesting beaches (visited in all by perhaps a thousand loggerheads) and a number of minor rookeries. Hotels and other tourist facilities have been built on many nesting beaches. At others the turtles have to negotiate a narrow channel of concrete tetrapods to reach the beach.

Since the 1970s Japan has witnessed an epidemic of tetrapods – four-legged constructions built to control sea currents. It is difficult to begrudge villagers flood protection or smart new harbours. Yet even stretches of coast recommended as beauty

Turtles are rarely sighted at sea but records of tagged hatchlings reveal that they begin their journey away from their natal beach by drifting northwards. The tiny tags, pinned through the edge of the shell, fall off as the shell grows.

Below: *On many stretches of coast, as far as the eye can see, ranks of tetrapods displace the interface between land and sea.*

spots are lined with tetrapods and concrete embankments. In a country where land is in short supply the coast is seen as having immense development potential. A guidebook to industry in the Ryukyu Islands is a case in point: 'The tropical sun, ocean and other elements endow Okinawa with rich natural resources for industry . . . large parts of the coastal area are in excellent condition for the establishment of seaside industrial regions; the existence of the great reef makes it easy to reclaim land.'

On Ishigaki Island a short stretch, perhaps 5 km, of reef and lagoon provides the fishermen of Shiraho village with at least fifty edible species of fish as well as octopus, cuttlefish, sea-urchins and lobsters. I spent a few days at Shiraho which, like other fishing villages, has lost many of its young men to the cities. The fishermen are ruled by the tides. Early one morning I watched as the spear fishermen came off the reef and two or three women arrived at the shore to help their husbands sort through the nets which had been set all night. They filled their bowls with tropical fish and packed them with ice. Then, resting one bowl on a towel wrapped around their head, and another in the crook of their arm, they took the best fish to the dealer from Okinawa and the rest to sell at the town market. Two old women came to pray at the two sacred rocks on the beach – like the wedded rocks at Ise, one was male, the other female. A few young children greeted the boats as they came in, clapping their hands in delight when they saw the big, colourful fish. The men went home to sleep and it was not until the afternoon that the harbour came to life again. Women came to collect shellfish and seaweed from the rocks while the tide was still low. Throughout the year the reef provides eight seaweed species which are used as food or fertilizer. A few fishermen

By the late 1970s more than half of the coastline of Japan's four main islands had been developed. By 1984 further development had left only 46 per cent in its natural state. In Okinawa, largest of the Ryukyu Islands, 80 per cent of the coral reef is now dead.

Mr and Mrs Taira sorting the catch from the nets that had been left on the Shiraho reef overnight. Shiraho is one of the few remaining sections of living reef in the Ryukyu Islands. In a survey of over three hundred sections of the reef Dr Katherine Muzik found only seventeen with more than 50 per cent of living coral.

Facing page: *Women from more than a hundred families still gather shellfish and at least eight seasonal varieties of seaweed from the shore or reef at Shiraho.*

waded out to spear octopus from the crevices. Others stayed on the beach to mend nets that had snagged on coral.

At Shiraho I was given a wonderful opportunity to observe a living coral reef. From above the corals looked blurred, a veiled pattern of shape and colour. Below the water I entered a new world. The beds of coral were separated by pools of bright white sand where sea-cucumbers trundled and in the shallow waters of the lagoon turtle grass billowed in the current. Corals, colonies of small sedentary animals called polyps which feed off plankton, have tiny single-celled plants living in their tissues which depend on sunlight to photosynthesize and provide the carbohydrates the corals use for growth. The main body of the reef comprises the hard calcareous exoskeleton built by the corals to protect themselves. I saw corals growing in many different ways: jagged and steep, furled like lettuces and branched like antlers; some spread flat like tables while others resembled fungi. The corals provide a platform to which other plants and animals attach. They in turn attract more creatures which find lairs and hiding places in the chasms and valleys of the reef. Gaudy butterfly, parrot and damsel fish dart in the sunlight

among the yellow, green, purple and blue living tissues of the coral. Shiraho is believed to have the largest stands of the rare blue coral *Heliopora coerulea* in Japan and perhaps in the world.

The people of Shiraho have been lucky. Much of the coral community around the Ryukyu Islands is dead, the reef grey and brown, buried in silt and glazed with a haze of algae. Unlike the clear waters of Shiraho lagoon, the waters are murky and any creature that stirs releases a cloud of dust – the precious red soil of the islands. Silt, the product of coastal tourist development and inland farming, has killed the coral.

Like the other islands in the Ryukyus, Ishigaki has been farmed on a small scale for years but recently, with the aid of government grants, vast areas of native forest have been felled to make way for dam construction and cash crops like pineapples and sugar cane. Devoid of its protective forest cover the topsoil washes away and from the air after heavy rain, red rivers can be seen sweeping into the blue sea. In Okinawa, the main island of the group, 80 per cent of the coral reef is already dead.

Vast areas of the Ryukyu Islands are no longer the tropical paradise that travel brochures make them out to be. And to boost the tourist trade the prefectural government is proposing to build a large airport, the land for which will be created by taking rock and soil from a nearby hill (Karadake) and dumping it in the lagoon over Shiraho coral reef. If the airport is built, one of the last living stretches of coral reef – and the fishermen's livelihood – will be buried beneath it. Ironically most of the pink coral and exotic shells sold to tourists in the Ryukyus now comes from Taiwan or the Philippines.

The seas around Japan can no longer supply the nation's needs. About 50 per cent of the country's animal protein supply still comes from fish, much of which is now caught in international or foreign waters. Japan catches or imports more than 15 per cent of the world's marine products, a larger share than any other nation. Her huge appetite has caused friction with fishermen from other countries. In the north Pacific, for example, her fleets trawl for pollack, drift nets for squid and salmon and catch much of the best tuna. In the process hundreds of other creatures are caught, many of which are wasted.

Japan also imports stuffed sea-turtles and sea-turtle products. The international commercial trade in sea-turtles is restricted by the Convention on International Trade in Endangered Species (CITES). All seven species are listed in the most at risk category, Appendix I, which implies that they are threatened with extinction and that trade cannot be justified. In practice, however, the effectiveness of CITES is limited. Restricted animals

Broken pieces of coral are used for jewellery and decoration. (Coral harvested on a small scale had a number of traditional uses – crushed coral was used as a kind of plaster for roof tiles.) Today most of the coral sold to tourists is imported from abroad. A 14-cm branched coral may sell for £300 while a good piece, 30 cm tall, can fetch over £1,500.

fetch higher prices and therefore boost local incomes. A member country is expected to monitor its own imports and exports but many of the ninety-three countries which have ratified CITES, particularly those with hundreds of islands, such as Indonesia, or with huge borders like Brazil, have neither the means to monitor poaching nor the internal legislation to prosecute offenders. CITES itself has no procedure by which it can penalize offending countries. A member country can place a reservation on any species it wishes, allowing it to continue trading.

Japan ratified CITES in 1980 and took reservations on three species of sea-turtle: the hawksbill, the green and the olive

Hawksbill and green sea-turtles, rare visitors to the Ryukyu Islands, are caught as they come to lay eggs and brought to this small workshop in Ishigaki to be stuffed.

Facing page: *Mrs Noriko Ezaki selects a flawless piece of tortoiseshell or* **bekko** *for the hull of the treasure ship shown on page 162.*

ridley. She imports stuffed turtles for the tourist industry, olive ridley and green turtle skins for the leather trade and hawksbill as raw shell for the tortoiseshell or *bekko* industry.

As symbolic gifts promising health and longevity, stuffed turtles have become a popular tourist souvenir in the south over the past decade. Most of the turtles on sale are now imported from countries such as Indonesia, Singapore and the Philippines. A green or hawksbill can fetch between £200 and £400. However, in the Ryukyu Islands some fishermen still catch the occasional turtle. On Ishigaki, for instance, while I was there a steady supply of green and loggerhead turtles and even rarer species was taken to the 'turtle taxidermist'.

Bekko is an ancient Japanese craft. It uses the thirteen large plates and the twenty-two edge pieces which make up the dark brown carapace and the twenty-three pale gold pieces from the underbelly or plastron of the hawksbill turtle. The loggerhead cannot be used for *bekko* because its carapace is too fragile so the material has to be imported. *Bekko* became particularly popular in the seventeenth century and while Japan was closed to outside trade tortoiseshell arrived through the only open

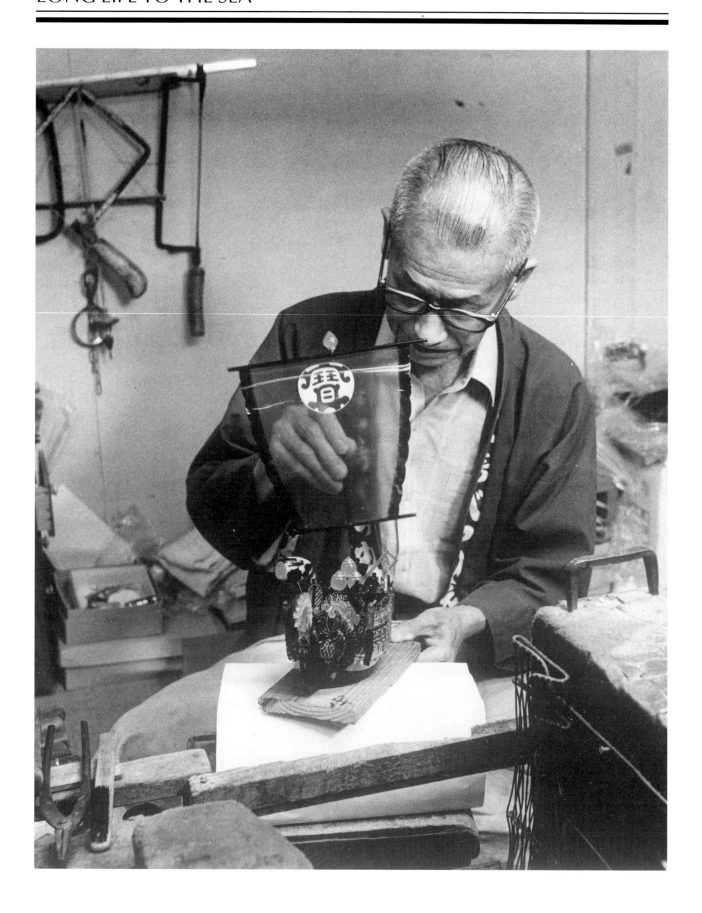

port, Nagasaki, which still remains the centre of the industry today.

I was shown how *bekko* is crafted by the Ezaki family. The grandfather, who is a seventh-generation master craftsman, first sketched a design of the legendary treasure ship. His daughter-in-law then selected a large, flawless piece of shell for the ship's hull. The fifteen or so craftsmen on the shop floor worked on the treasures and sails, made from the more valuable underbelly pieces. Each piece was cleaned and shaved, clamped between wood to flatten it and then cut to shape. Pieces were fused by clamping them in hot tongs and dousing them in cold water. It was impossible to recognize any join. After heating and sanding the golden parts turned translucent, revealing an astonishing depth of colour. In the final stages the pieces were delicately carved by hand, then polished and fitted into the treasure ship. The Ezakis showed me some exquisite pieces: a crane with a chick, a falcon, a samurai helmet, a carp climbing a waterfall, a caged bird, and a complete *bekko* cabinet commissioned by the imperial family.

While I was there coachloads of tourists crowded into the showroom to examine tie-pins, cufflinks, hair ornaments and jewellery. In the early 1960s the *bekko* industry began to wane but it found new custom designing modern hair ornaments and attracting the luxury fashion market with spectacle frames and expensive jewellery. According to the Bekko Association there are about a hundred independent companies in Nagasaki including some people who have set up on their own to supply special commissions. Some conservationists claim that a few of these businesses have machines which stamp out pieces of *bekko* on a conveyor belt and although they find it difficult to deny hand-skilled craftsmen their trade, they would like to outlaw machines which eat through large amounts of material using relatively unskilled labour. The Bekko Association, confident in its role of preserving an important and respected part of Japanese culture, responds by saying that all work with *bekko* requires skilled craftsmen and provides jobs.

The third industry which imports turtle products, the leather industry, lacks the aristocratic status enjoyed by the Bekko Association. Turtle is just one of many leathers used in the small but significant fashion market for items such as shoes and handbags. I was shown a warehouse which stocked elephant, Cayman (a kind of alligator), ostrich, snake and lizard leather. Apparently, turtle leather is not one of the most prized. With only a fifth of the value of the best crocodile skin, it was used as an alternative when crocodiles became more difficult to import

The finished treasure ship created entirely from raw **bekko** *or tortoiseshell without the use of glue. The ship carries a cargo of treasure for the seven lucky gods, a barrel of rice, a magic cape, a key, a lucky hammer, an inexhaustible purse, coral or other jewels, and a fan.*

Young people are no longer interested in the traditional tortoiseshell hair combs. The bekko industry has tried to attract this market by producing modern designs for items such as brooches costing between £40 and £150.

in the 1960s. Compared to a crocodile, each turtle yields only a small amount of leather: from the skin around the flippers and neck. I was introduced to a couple who worked as a team skilfully stitching the traditional *zori* (special shoes that are worn with the kimono at important ceremonies) from turtle leather dyed a rich wine colour. I was also shown the process by which animal skin is turned into leather. First it is shaved to remove traces of animal fat, scales or other materials. The pieces are then tanned in a huge revolving drum before being stitched, dyed, stretched, sprayed with preservatives and other chemicals and finally polished.

For different reasons the leather industry is as powerful as the Bekko Association in its fight to maintain a supply of raw materials. Despite the abolition of the class system in 1868, for a few Japanese class divisions and prejudices run deep. In medieval Japan, because of the Buddhist ethic against harming animals, handling them was considered the lowliest of tasks and at the bottom of the class system were a people officially classified as non-persons. They comprised outcasts and feudal refugees working as butchers, tanners and waste-collectors, all tasks shunned by the rest of the community. Today, although most Japanese consider the old class system forgotten, some families are at a disadvantage because of the residual effects of discrimination and fear that the right-wing movement may encourage the government to dispose of the special laws that protect them. A liberation league has been formed to help those whose jobs or marriage prospects are affected. In the present political climate, there is pressure on the government to maintain the imports of exotic leather which remain important to these people's livelihood. And the distributors and retailers of the prosperous fashion industry are adding to the demand to retain the leather supply.

Well aware of the growing international pressure to halt the trade in sea-turtles, both the leather and *bekko* industries have been studying proposals for rearing turtles in captivity on other Pacific islands where they breed naturally. Japan already has one turtle hatchery in the Bonin Islands and is supporting another in the Palau Islands off the Philippines. The aim of these hatcheries is to support the conservation of sea-turtles by taking eggs from the wild, then hatching and rearing them for a few weeks in captivity to give them a 'head start' before releasing them. Thus they avoid the early vulnerable period when so many hatchlings are taken by predators.

For their part, conservationists are generally wary of hatchery proposals for three reasons. Most importantly eggs have to be taken from the wild: no one is yet breeding second-generation turtles successfully in captivity. Secondly so many biological questions remain unanswered: no one yet knows whether 'head-started' turtles pick up the signals they need in order to find their way back to the breeding beaches. Thirdly some fear that the turtle-based industries might in the future have commercial designs on the hatcheries, and open new markets for turtle products while wild turtle populations are still endangered.

Japan remains the world's biggest importer of turtle products. France, which initially placed reservations on the green and hawksbill, and Italy on the green, both withdrew in 1984 leaving only Surinam and Japan with reservations. After signing CITES Japan set an annual import limit of 30 tonnes of raw tortoiseshell, representing some 30,000 hawksbills. In 1985 the stuffed-turtle industry imported 14,137 kg of turtle; an estimated 10,000 to 18,000 juvenile hawksbills according to the Washington-based Sea-turtle Rescue Fund, while the leather industry imported 26,130 kg of raw skins accounting for 50 to 80,000 olive ridley and green sea-turtles. But all these figures show a significant decrease in trade since Japan signed CITES. In the 1970s Japan imported hawksbill products from more than forty-seven countries; in 1984 she imported from only twenty-one, nine of which were party to CITES. The doors are gradually closing.

*   *   *

It has been whales rather than turtles, however, that have been the subject of the greatest international outcry. Fishing tools found in ancient Jōmon settlements include a primitive harpoon which was probably used to hunt sea-lions, seals and small cetaceans such as dolphins and pilot whales. By the end of the Heian period whales had become an important food source in isolated towns such as Taiji on the southern coast of the Kii peninsula. In the seventeenth century an ingenious method of fishing was devised at Taiji which allowed the capture of larger whales, ranging from the minke to the sperm whale, humpbacks and fin whales. A scout on the clifftop hoisted a flag to signal the type of whale sighted and then, using different flags, he guided crews of rowing boats which surrounded the whale with a large net. Three black-and-white striped flags indicated a right whale with her calf, an instruction to turn back, since a whale with a calf was taboo. Like a fly caught in a spider's web, the whale thrashed in the net until exhausted, and the whalers moved in for the kill. The industry prospered and the method spread to other coastal villages. During this period Taiji took about a hundred whales a year.

The best cuts of meat were sent to the courts in Kyoto and Edo. Among the aristocrats the Buddhist ethic against killing animals generally prevailed and gradually, as transport became easier, the whale, which was regarded as a fish, became a more widely accepted meat. The villagers found a use for every part. Whale blubber was turned into oil for fuel or mixed with vinegar and sold to control insects in the rice paddies. Oil obtained from bones was used for cooking and making soap. The gut, tendons and sinews were used to lash wood together or for armour. The baleen, a horny material from the whale's palate but known as whalebone, was worked into tips of fishing rods, pipes, and puppet springs, and whale tooth was fashioned into tools and ornaments. Those parts of the entrails which were not eaten were boiled down to make stock for soup. Any unused material was subsequently turned into fertilizer. There was even a saying in Taiji that one whale would keep seven villages through an entire winter.

At the beginning of the nineteenth century the foreign whaling ships arrived. By the 1850s, Russia, Britain, America, Holland

In 1677 Yoritomo Wada invented the technique of catching large whales by surrounding them with a ring of nets (made in those days from rice straw) at Taiji, a small village in Wakayama prefecture. He is said to have got the idea from watching a spider catch flies in a web. (Taiji Whale Museum, Japan)

and France were concentrating much of their whaling fleet, totalling seven hundred or so ships, in the waters around Japan. These western whalers killed primarily for oil. Although they used some baleen and whale teeth, generally the rest was wasted. As whales became scarce many coastal towns were forced to give up whaling. The people of Taiji returned to hunting the small cetaceans, dolphins and pilot whales, rounding them up by boat and driving them into a bay where they could be slaughtered.

But large whales had been Taiji's livelihood and in December 1885 one of her leaders gave the order to hunt a right whale and calf. No one in Taiji is allowed to forget what followed. Trapped in the net the whale fought furiously, trying to save her calf. Helped by the winds and current she dragged the boats out to sea. Next morning, the desperate whalers cut the nets loose but it was too late, both for them and the whale. About 110 men, the pride of Taiji's whaling fleet, perished.

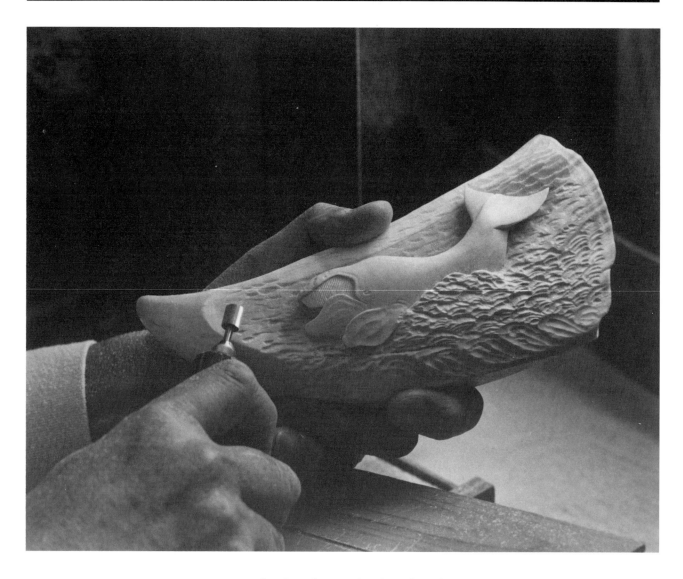

Carving the tooth or 'ivory' of a sperm whale, the largest of the toothed whales. Today about five thousand people, including whalers, flensers, craftsmen and people who work in the offices of whaling companies, obtain their living in the whaling industry.

In the aftermath of such a disaster Taiji was ready to give up whaling. But somebody had learned in America how to use a gun-fired harpoon and this method was developed, enabling individual boats to pursue whales. Other towns, such as Ayukawa on the northeast coast of Honshu, adopted the technique and once more the industry prospered. By the early twentieth century Japan had become a naval power and her whalers were able to buy big ships fitted with harpoons from great whaling nations such as Norway. They turned from commercial offshore or coastal whaling to deep-sea or pelagic whaling. In 1934 the first Japanese ships went to the Antarctic, many crewed by men from Taiji and Ayukawa. The industry continued to prosper and in postwar Japan whale meat became a cheap source of protein and many people tasted it for the first time.

Japan now had seven fleets in the Antarctic. Each September

Taiji and Ayukawa held religious services for the departing whalers, praying for their safe return the following spring. The mother or factory ships sailed from ports such as Yokohama south of Tokyo and Shiminoseki near Hiroshima. Once in good whaling territory twenty or so catcher boats worked to one mother ship bringing in anything from ten to fifty whales a day. The whales were then cut up and the meat processed and frozen aboard the factory ships. As the Japanese competed with the Netherlands, England, Norway and Russia, the Antarctic waters became a free for all.

In 1946 the International Whaling Commission (IWC) was set up, its function being to maintain stocks of the great whale species and to regulate the whaling industry. Although it is not an anti-whaling conservation body, it does exert control by limiting the whaling season, setting catch quotas and banning the whaling of some species. Decisions depend on a three-quarters majority of members. In its early days, when most members were whaling nations and any that lodged an objection within ninety days were then not obliged to abide by a council ruling, the IWC was accused of being totally ineffective. Since then the public pressure movement, led by Greenpeace, has encouraged more and more governments to take an anti-whaling stance. To date roughly three-quarters of IWC members are non-whaling and in 1982 members voted to suspend commercial whaling from 1986 by setting zero catch limits for all the species of great whales. The reasoning behind this was that the IWC did not have sufficiently accurate scientific data to be sure that it was setting reasonable and safe catch limits and too many species were running close to the critical level.

Japan lodged an objection within the required ninety days, which she subsequently withdrew in July 1986. To allow her crews to continue whaling in the 1987 season, she agreed to stop commercial pelagic whaling on 1 May 1987, to stop commercial coastal whaling for minke and Bryde's whale on 1 October 1987 and commercial coastal sperm whaling by 1 April 1988. The statement concluded by saying that this agreement would lapse if at any time before April 1988 a United States Court required certain amendments to be put in motion. This referred to a remarkable clause, built into an American conservation act of 1979, whereby any country responsible for diminishing the effectiveness of international agreements is liable to American sanctions. Activated against Japan it would mean that Japanese fishing in American waters could be cut by half. This would have a far more catastrophic effect on Japan's economy than the loss of the whaling industry. Squeezed into a tight corner, Japan

Fishing tackle at Taiji. The whalers were once the cream of Taiji's fishing fleet but many now recognize that whaling is a dying way of life.

made a private agreement with America to stop commercial whaling by 1986/7 provided that America did not activate sanctions. The US government was taken to court by conservation bodies who maintained that the agreement was unlawful. The conservationists finally lost their case and have generally decided to sit back and see what happens.

Thus Japan's agreement to stop commercial whaling has not come about through any resolve of her own or pressure from her own people but because the threat of sanctions put her in a no-win situation. Understanding this makes it easier to appreciate the attitudes of the Japanese which is crucially important because the IWC has promised to review the quotas in 1990. There are many millions of Japanese who do not eat whale and who would be unaffected if Japan stopped whaling. Yet press reports suggest that an increasing number of Japanese are angry at what they see as unprecedented outside criticism and pressure. This anger has converted many previously neutral people into a pro-whaling position. The anti-whaling lobby has been accused of using whales to express an anti-Japanese stance. Some people believe that Japan should stop whaling simply to protect her international image. But generally the Japanese question the right of other countries to criticize them when they have taken thousands of whales from Japan's coastal waters in previous years. In addition they ask why westerners should dictate what the Japanese, who have always lived off the sea, eat, especially when westerners consume far more red meat than the Japanese do. To illustrate the Japanese demand for whale meat they point out that because of restrictions they have had to import from countries such as Norway, Iceland and Korea.

The whalers emphasize the loss of jobs and as a group feel they have been unfairly maligned. They say that other countries could afford to stop whaling because they no longer needed the oil. The Japanese, they say, have a greater respect for the whale than any other country, erecting tombs and holding ceremonies to pray for the souls of the whales they have caught. They stress that the whales are killed as humanely and quickly as possible and that they keep careful scientific records of the number of whales caught. They insist that there are plenty of some species of whales in the Antarctic and that the numbers taken are strictly controlled since it is obviously in their own best interest to prevent such an important resource from becoming extinct.

The Japanese are realizing that, although the IWC attempts to base its guidelines on scientific knowledge of population numbers, much of the enormous international public pressure is driven by emotion. Reports suggest that a few Japanese have indicated they will do their best to keep the whale industry going in one form or another during the moratorium. A few pro-whaling people have pointed out that Iceland and Korea are continuing to whale under scientific permit and that North American Inuit are still whaling because they have been placed in a subsistence category. At the same time they realize that if Japan attempted to pursue either policy her motives would be questioned by conservationists. It is generally thought that Japan will probably increase the catches of smaller dolphins and pilot whales which at present are not controlled by the IWC. Although the method of whaling is entirely different, the meat provided could help to keep the market open for a possible return to the large whaling.

I first went to Taiji in April 1985 at the end of the dolphin fishing season. Eight or so dolphins were swimming in the bay. A net, marked by gaily coloured floats, prevented them from returning to the open sea. The scene was peaceful and there was no sign of a tetrapod along the tree-clad coast. I was told that one of the dolphins was destined for the aquarium in the marine park in the next bay.

I returned to Taiji in October when the fishing season was just under way. The bay was tightly packed with several hundred euphrosyne dolphins. The next day a boat moved in among them before turning out of sight into a little bay. I walked along the path and looked round the corner. Two metres or so in front of me a man in a wet suit was hauling aboard the dolphin he had just slaughtered. Three dead dolphins lay in the boat, their paler bellies pointing upwards. Later I learned that the dolphins were slaughtered individually, their throats slit with a knife under water, but all I took in then was that the sea was red, an image that remains with me. Within ten minutes the blood had started to seep into the main bay, a red tide to smother the green. The dolphins in the bay, sensing danger, began to swim in tight circles, leaping and thrashing against the holding net. Some leapt over the first net but did not have room to gather momentum to leap the second. One dolphin caught its fin. It struggled hard for about five minutes then every now and again thrashed its tail before it finally submerged.

A number of tourists had stopped to watch. One or two enterprising taxi drivers had been able to show their passengers the whole event by whizzing them back and forth along the coast road. The fishermen made no attempt to hide their work. Later I returned to watch them unfurling the net. The pool of blood began to seep through the gap and into the open sea. The dolphin that had drowned in the net was lifted into the boat. I followed the boats round to a harbour shed where the dolphins were disembowelled, their meat cut, stacked and loaded into a lorry.

The next day I watched as a school of perhaps four or five hundred short-finned pilot whales (*Globicephala macrorhynchus*) were driven into the same bay. They panicked when they found they were trapped in the shallow water. Mothers vainly tried to protect their calves but the sea was full of thrashing bodies. Those closest to the shore were pushed against the rocks. As their tails writhed in an effort to escape, the rocks cut like razors and again blood flowed into the sea.

In three days I had seen about eight hundred small whales captured for slaughter in Taiji. I tried to find out how many small cetaceans were taken each year. One figure I was given was three thousand. The season, restricted voluntarily, runs between October and April and I was assured that many days go by without any sightings. These catches of small whales are not considered real whaling by the townspeople, although they have always resorted to this method in times of hardship. Friends of the Earth Japan estimates that each year as many as

When this picture was taken the slaughter of these pilot whales had not begun. They were kept in the bay until the meat from the dolphin slaughter (see page 174) had been processed. The blood in the sea came from the pilot whales which, trapped in shallow water, were pushed against the razor-sharp rocks.

thirty thousand small cetaceans (including those destroyed because they compete with fishermen) are killed around the coast. Very little is known about the numbers of the various species of small cetaceans but some people believe that this fishery is not exploited to its full potential. If so, then in many people's opinion, this type of whaling is not a conservation problem.

Next to the 'killing bay' at Taiji is an aquarium with performing dolphins and pilot whales. Tourists can watch both spectacles in one day. Dolphins belong to the whale family but I learned that many Japanese make a clear distinction between dolphins and whales. A number of people expressed shock at the thought of eating dolphin, since it was an intelligent creature they had come to love and respect. Some dolphins, like those killed at Iki island because they competed for fish, are used for fertilizer. Most dolphins, however, are hunted for their meat, much of which is eaten locally but research suggests that some of it is being sold in city markets as 'whale meat'. For as long as commercial exploitation of the great whale species is officially banned, it is the meat of the small cetaceans which is likely to find its way into many more markets.

Many Japanese, like westerners, are dolphin lovers and would be shocked at the thought of eating dolphin. Yet in about 10 areas around the coast dolphins like these euphrosynes or blue-whites **(Stenella coeruleoalba)** *are killed for their meat.*

There is a small but dedicated anti-whaling movement in Japan and I quote from an article written by a Japanese member:

After more than ten years of focusing on Japan . . . the international movement has largely failed to move the Japanese people. Each separate effort to 'educate' Japanese has been like a foray into alien territory, with little regard for the reality of the situation in Japan . . . Any environmental group which is against whaling in Japan has to be ready for ridicule and criticism by the mass media and non-cooperation or hostility from other organizations. The most common epithet is to call them stooges of anti-Japanese westerners. The whaling issue is too controversial and the stakes too high to make an aggressive commitment. The Japanese conservation movement is in its infancy and you cannot expect a baby to carry fire.

Whaling is not generally seen as an ecological issue about a rare species but as an issue of economics, emotions and, above all, national pride.

As more and more doors are closed on international trade, the Japanese may have to increase the exploitation of their own wildlife. Some conservationists fear the people will become increasingly angry and alienated by international pressure, causing more damage to wildlife. They would like to nurture the kind of resistance put forward by the fishermen of Taiji who have fought long and hard against large-scale development which has ruined so many other parts of the coastline. Yet whaling provides a livelihood for many Taiji people and they fear that if they give it up another important industry – the valuable tourist trade – will be lost. In fact Taiji, which has the strongest history of all the whaling towns, a good museum and an aquarium with performing small whales and dolphins, might attract even more interest if Japan stops whaling. In America taking tourists to view whales off the coast is a growing business; however the proud Japanese whalers might not be content with looking after tourists. For the present Taiji is doing all it can to to get the message across that they need to continue whaling. A festival in honour of the whale is celebrated every summer. Clad in the traditional whalers' red loincloths, the boys of Taiji dance on a platform of two ancient whale boats singing about the glories of whaling.

By contrast the children of another fishing village dance each summer to celebrate the turtles they have protected. School-children from the small town of Hiwasa on the west coast of Shikoku, worried about the effects of hunters and egg thieves after the war, began protecting turtles in the 1950s. They cleared rubbish from the beach and guarded the turtles when they came to lay. They received a prize for their work, and news spread that Hiwasa was taking the unprecedented step of protecting its turtles. The town office decided to take charge. Taking Dr Uchida's advice, the harbour lights are turned off during the hatching season and the people shut their curtains so that the hatchlings are not confused in their orientation towards the sea. Visitors come from as far as Osaka to watch the magic of turtles laying eggs. The town asked the government to make their beach a national monument giving it official wildlife protection status. In 1985 a sea-turtle museum was opened and it is hoped that international sea-turtle conferences will be held there. The decision to protect the turtles has both boosted the tourist industry and brought fame and prosperity to Hiwasa.

Each summer Hiwasa holds a festival in honour of Urashima Taro. A boy on a turtle float leads the procession and turtles are released into the sea. The tale of Urashima Taro has a cautionary ending. Believing he has spent three years in the sea, Urashima

In the past at Taiji whalers danced on a bridge between two boats lashed together in the sea before each season began. The whale song has been performed in other parts of Japan as part of Taiji's effort to preserve its culture and convey the message that it needs to continue whaling.

Facing page: 'Monkey trainer on turtle looking at the distant palace of the Dragon King'. The man on the turtle is Urashima Taro on his underwater journey. This picture by Shinsai (c. 1820) may be the frontispiece for a set of prints based on the legend. (Chester Beatty Library)

asks the sea goddess if he can go back to his home village one last time before he commits himself to life in the underwater world. The goddess gives him a casket but begs him not to open it. The sea-turtle carries him back to his village but it looks strange and the people do not recognize him. Longing for the delights of the sea he opens the casket. Urashima finds himself rapidly turning into a wizened old man. The three years were really three hundred. The lesson is about greed. The turtle may be the symbol of longevity and a lucky omen for a good harvest but the people know that the creatures of the sea are not immortal. Today the sea-turtle no longer breeds at Urashima's home in the Tango peninsula.

文字関垣

喜多嶋たこの
龍「蓬蘂砂
亀まひかれて
心よく猿曳

四方歌垣
其秋

猿曳ハ波の白馬ニ言フ
珍の郡の龙るらる人

177

THE HOPE AND THE FUTURE

In a quick decision
I cut off my tail
I believed this had saved my life
But now I fear that my tail
Left behind at that site
Was the real me
And what survives
Is only a shrivelled skin
This feeling strikes me
Like a leather whip.

The Lizard *by Hiroko Kagawa 1969*
translated by Miwako Kurosaka and Alfred Birnbaum

Japan's continued exploitation of threatened wildlife species remains a major concern to world conservationists. Japan ratified CITES in 1980 but placed 'reservations' (exemptions which allow the continuation of trading) on fourteen of the species listed in Appendix I, the category most at risk. This, the highest number of reservations taken by any CITES member, justifies the accusation that Japan is the world's largest trader in endangered species. As well as six whales and three sea-turtles, the exemptions include the musk deer (*Moschus moschiferus*), the saltwater crocodile (*Crocodylus porosus*) and the yellow, desert and Bengal monitor lizards: *Varanus flavescens*, *V. griseus* and *V. bengalensis*. Japan also continues to trade in other Appendix I species on which she has not placed reservations.

Japan's trade in endangered species supplies raw materials for oriental medicine and the ancient leather and ivory crafts. A desire for western status symbols, such as fur coats, snake- and crocodile-skin handbags and shoes, has increased this trade. The Japanese traditionally collect goldfish and songbirds, but nowadays many people also want to keep exotic parrots and

Traditional and modern side by side. Both the zori *– ceremonial shoes worn with the kimono – and the handbag, a western status symbol, depend on trade in animal species whose wild populations are threatened.*

Previous page: *Early morning commuters waiting to catch a train at Shinjuku station, Tokyo. Unlikely to leave work before 7 or 8 p.m., then expected to socialize with their colleagues, it will be midnight before many of the businessmen return home.*

fish, orchids, cacti and even primates.

There is a large turnover in the trade in exotic species partly because many die so easily. Some perish during transport and others, like cacti from arid countries, find Japan's rainy season too humid, while primates and parrots from tropical countries find the winters too cold. The individual species names of imported cacti, parrots and primates are often not listed, making it extremely difficult for the authorities to keep a check on the situation. But sales lists give evidence that at least twenty species of cacti listed on CITES Appendix I are regularly sold. Colourful parrots are popular pets and data collected from importers in 1981 listed over 100,000 parrots representing 107 species listed in the various categories of CITES.

The Japanese are passionate collectors and as new and interesting fish species are discovered, dealers make them available. The black arowana, which is not a protected species, was on sale in Japan the year after it was discovered. Spotted barramunids from Indonesia appeared on sale a year after they had been officially protected.

Japan also imports nine Appendix I species of fish, most of which arrive with documents classing them as 'captive bred'. But TRAFFIC-Japan, a branch of an international organization set up by the World Wildlife Fund to monitor trade in threatened species, believes many are caught in the wild.

Partly because of their artistic inheritance and partly because of the shortage of space, people are drawn to the bizarre or the small. Japanese department stores are world leaders in the art of creating shows to attract customers. Fish are popular in summer exhibitions with titles such as 'Strange Fish' and 'Amazon Show'. In 1984 a craze for frilled lizards was sparked off by a television commercial. In 1986, the Year of the Tiger, a tiger was found on exhibition in a department store in Shikoku.

TRAFFIC is increasingly worried about the trade in primates originating from Thailand and Bolivia, despite the fact that these countries have export bans on their threatened primates. By monitoring pet shops in Tokyo TRAFFIC uncovered a regular trade in white-handed and white-cheeked gibbons, both Appendix I species. Customs officers have found primates in the hand luggage of Japanese tourists returning from Thailand and other Southeast Asian countries. One such smuggler carried eleven primates in his hand luggage, five of which were dead; he was neither prosecuted nor fined. The animals were simply confiscated and put in zoos. While I was in Japan TRAFFIC was attempting to trace a consignment of fourteen golden-headed tamarins, one of the rarest monkeys in the world, which had

THE HOPE AND THE FUTURE

White-cheeked gibbon in a warehouse in Osaka. This species is listed in Appendix I of CITES, an agreement which regulates trade in endangered species. Tourists returning from Asian countries have been found with primates in their hand luggage. In December 1986 the government promised to introduce new legislation to make CITES more effective.

been smuggled into the country to be sold to zoos. None of the owners of pet shops where TRAFFIC has found Appendix I species have been prosecuted since there is no domestic legislation for prosecution or confiscation of wildlife once it is safely in Japan. TRAFFIC operates primarily in Tokyo but cities such as Osaka and Kobe are known to be more active centres of animal trading. Most of the dealers are aware of CITES regulations and are therefore wary of foreigners but as my researcher discovered in Osaka, if you are a Japanese person it is relatively easy to be promised the animal you want, simply by picking up the telephone directory.

The raw materials needed for oriental medicine are generally extracted in their country of origin. Musk comes from a golfball-size pod in the anal gland of the male musk deer which it uses to mark its territory. Wild musk is usually obtained by killing the deer and 40 adult deer provide only 1 kg. The Himalayan population of the musk deer is on Appendix I of CITES and lives in the mountainous regions straddling Nepal, India, Afghanistan and Pakistan. Samurai used to carry pouches of musk into battle and today it is sold as a remedy for heart disease and sexual disorders, to improve stamina and sexual performance and, blended with ginseng, gall bladder and deer horn, as a popular tonic for children with colic. Japan consumes 80 per cent of the world's supply of musk and, as she has placed reservations, she is by the rules of CITES entitled to do so. Virtually all the countries with wild musk deer have signed agreements banning exports, yet Japan continues to receive wild musk. Hong Kong recently tightened its controls on musk, leaving Japan's open market the one big thorn in the international campaign to save the musk deer. In the anticipation of more doors closing musk imports rocketed to 473 kg in 1985. However, there are signs that Japan is bowing to international opinion. The government has recently issued 'guidance' that musk should be used only in traditional medicine and they anticipate that this will reduce consumption by as much as 40 per cent.

Gall bladder is taken from the Asiatic black bear which is also in Appendix I of CITES. It is used for digestive and inflammatory problems. Japan did not place a reservation on international trade because she has wild black bears of her own. The black bear can be captured or killed by licensed game hunters and can be shot as a pest in areas where it feeds in plantations and causes 'problems' for foresters. In the 1980s TRAFFIC discovered that large numbers of Japan's bears, officially destined for South Korean zoos, were actually supplying the Korean gall bladder trade. The price of adult bears had risen to about £2,000. Since most of the available gall bladder is sold to South Korea, Japanese traders continue to import their gall bladder from other Asian

The oriental medicine stall at Takayama morning market. Monkey skull is used to cure 'nerves' and women's illnesses, snake as an aphrodisiac and the hanging dried lizards to stop bed-wetting and coughs.

ハブ酒 47° 1.5ℓ

うるま
¥15,000

Snakes pickled in sake as an aphrodisiac, on sale for tourists at Okinawa airport at £60 a jar.

countries, thereby breaking CITES regulations. Between 1978 and 1984 customs data shows that gall bladder imports account for an estimated forty thousand bears.

A number of traditional crafts depend on animal products for their raw materials. Japan placed reservations on the monitor lizard and the salt-water crocodile to provide skins for the leather industry. She continues to accept leather from countries such as Indonesia which have, by signing CITES, agreed to stop trading in these species. Japan's general attitude is that since she has placed reservations the fault lies with the exporter. Yet Japan also imports the leather of species such as the Siamese crocodile (*Crocodylus siamensis*) on which she has not placed a reservation. Trade in crocodile skin increased by 50 per cent between 1983 and 1985. The European countries have now withdrawn their earlier reservations and once again Japan is keeping the trade active.

Japan placed no reservations on rhinos or elephants, despite the fact that rhino horn is used in oriental medicine and finished ivory products have a yearly retail value of over £150 million. When Japan opened up to the West ivory *netsuke* (miniature sculptures, worn as decorative toggles on a kimono), hair ornaments, dishes and figurines were eagerly bought by foreigners. At the beginning of the twentieth century Britain was the biggest importer of ivory sculptures and by 1920 was supplying Japan with almost half of her raw ivory. By the 1970s Japan was importing an average of 463 tonnes a year and had become the world's greatest consumer of ivory products, a position retained today. Around 40 per cent of the ivory is used to make personalized seals for individual and company use. Signatures are rarely written. Instead a person carries three seals: one for personal use, another for more formal papers and a third which is legally binding; businesses require many more. Seals are also carved from wood, crystal and buffalo horn but ivory remains the most prestigious material. The seals are prepared in factories but the hallmark is carved by hand, an industry employing some 2,000 or more craftsmen. Only 5 per cent of the ivory is fashioned into *netsuke* or figurines, most of which are still bought by foreign collectors. The remaining ivory is used for jewellery, musical instruments and items such as ear picks and chopsticks.

Before CITES came into force Japanese dealers stockpiled and afterwards continued to buy poached ivory from countries such as the Sudan and Burundi. However, with the introduction in 1985 of an international quota system for ivory, Japan finally revised her laws so that only legal ivory could enter. For the first time Japan began to turn shipments of ivory away from her shores. CITES now believes that the controls are working effectively. Japanese dealers say they are in favour of stamping out poaching. If elephant populations are controlled 'officially' then in theory the ivory carvers will be able to obtain a stable supply of legal ivory as can already be done from countries with stockpiles or those such as Zimbabwe which are culling their elephants. For CITES, Japan's use of legal rather than illegal ivory is a step in the right direction.

There are other signs of hope on the international trade front. After signing CITES the Japanese government instructed pharmacists to stop using rhino horn (prescribed to strengthen the heart and reduce fever in oriental medicine). In 1986 a World

Ivory netsuke *of a monkey climbing bamboo, carved by Hoshunsai Masayuki c. 1870. About three hundred master craftsmen still work from home using hand tools only to create* netsuke *and other sculptures. Apprenticeship takes ten years.*

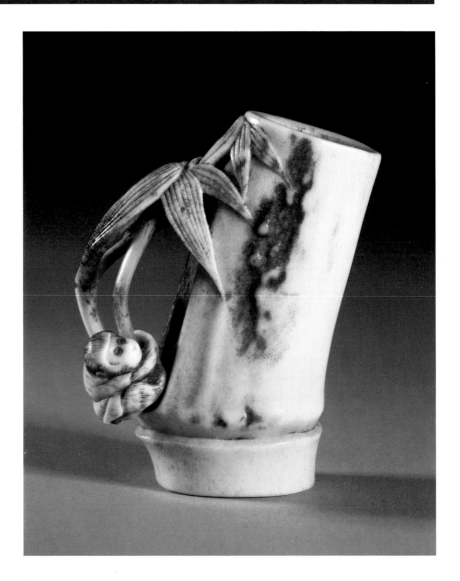

Wildlife Fund survey showed that in Tokyo, over six years the use of rhino horn in medicine had dropped by about a third. As pharmacists use up their old stock of rhino horn they are switching to substitutes such as the antlers of the Saiga antelope, and the government believes that imports of rhino horn have ceased.

The Japanese television service NHK recently highlighted the problems of the bear gall bladder trade in a pioneering pro-conservation film and there is some evidence that the trade in live black bears has slowed. In December 1986 the government promised to introduce new legislation to make CITES more effective. The fact that a TRAFFIC office exists and works in Japan is itself a milestone. When it was founded in 1982 it was hailed as a turning point for conservation in Asia.

Yet TRAFFIC, an international organization whose Japanese

office is run by Tom Milliken, an American conservationist, highlights the fact that much of the pressure to save Japan's wildlife still comes from abroad. As well as CITES, Japan has signed a number of international treaties including the Ramsar Convention (by which countries agree to nominate wetlands of international importance) and various treaties associated with migratory birds. But like CITES many of these are not backed up by the domestic legislation needed to make them effective. While western conservation pressure closes many possible trade routes, Japan's traders could continue to get most of the animals and products they want from the developing countries. Japanese tourists are already buying worked ivory from countries where labour costs are cheaper: seals from Burma and Taiwan and ornaments from Hong Kong and China. They also buy stuffed turtles from the Philippines. Trade will continue for as long as the Japanese will buy. Ultimately conservation is unlikely to succeed unless the demand for wildlife protection comes from the people themselves.

The first pockets of resistance to habitat loss within Japan emerged when local groups objected to development that threatened their own livelihoods. Then in 1951 the Nature Conservation Society of Japan was formed by a group of climbers, scholars and naturalists who had earlier joined forces to protect two favourite beauty spots, Me-Akandake in Hokkaido and part of Nikko National Park. But in the 1950s and early 1960s when Japan's economy was growing at a furious pace and development of industry and tourism was welcomed everywhere, most people kept to themselves any misgivings for the good of their country. Japan was still smarting from the shock of defeat in war and only something drastic could undermine her dedication to progress and prosperity. In 1959 thousands of people living around Minamata Bay in the Inland Sea were poisoned by eating fish contaminated with the mercury from a chemical factory. The tragedy of the poisoned people, locked into uncontrollable shuddering, was shown vividly on television. A spate of pollution scares followed and by the end of the 1960s laws were tightened. A number of rivers were cleaned up and the children's cry, 'Come back baby salmon', as they released salmon fry into rivers publicized the campaign. Today, close to Shibuya station in the heart of Tokyo a monitor continuously indicates a figure for the level of pollutants in the air.

The phrase 'nature conservation' gradually came into general use from about the mid 1960s. In 1970 the first nature conservation demonstration was staged in Tokyo and a year later the Japanese Union for Nature Conservation amalgamated the various small

The bullet train which travels at a maximum speed of 240 km per hour. In the background Fujisan is hidden in cloud and smog.

groups which had formed to protect small niches of hills or rivers. In the same year the chairman of one group blocked the outflow pipe of a pulp factory with cement. With the setting up of the Environment Agency, also in 1971, the future of nature conservation looked promising.

Since the mid 1970s progress, at least on an official level, has slowed down. An employee who has worked at the Environment Agency since it was founded once admitted that the early mood of dynamic commitment had been lost. He wasn't sure whether this was because nature conservation had been successful and there was less destruction to worry about, or whether people themselves were less concerned. During my travels around Japan I saw plenty of environmental destruction: the excavation of new mountains, the straightening of rivers, the clear felling of forests, the drainage and reclamation of wild land, even within national parks, or close to areas where, for instance, red-crowned cranes are known to breed. The labourers were proud of their work, with no sense (as there is in the West) that what they were doing is unpopular. So perhaps people are less concerned. But the voluntary conservation movement has not disappeared,

Oi bird sanctuary on the western shore of Tokyo bay, managed voluntarily by the Wild Bird Society. Close to Haneda, Tokyo's central airport, and flanked by heavy industry and a network of flyways, nevertheless, Oi is one of Tokyo's best spots for watching waterfowl.

it simply has not grown in the way that was expected at its inception.

In the late 1970s falling oil prices and other problems caused Japan's economy to slow down, forcing her to abandon some of the most ambitious schemes for development. Even so, industrial growth, which had brought Japan international recognition after the war, is still seen as the answer to economic problems. Because of lack of natural resources, economic survival is believed to lie with Japan's ability to turn raw imports into exports and, therefore, the manufacturing industries are vital. But with high standards of living and growing wage costs, Japan faces increasing

Tetrapods or concrete embankments line not only the coast but also creep inland along the rivers. To the conservationist, it seems that Japan has a limitless purse for 'public works' and improvement schemes.

competition from countries such as South Korea and Taiwan.

Pressure to relax or abolish expensive environmental controls has been successful. In 1978 the Environment Agency raised the acceptable level of nitrogen dioxide pollution from 0.02 parts per million to 0.05 ppm. The scientists who discovered the connection between mercury-contaminated fish and poisoned victims are not national heroes. Many families are still fighting for compensation. In 1982 the Liberal Democratic party actually petitioned to close the Environment Agency. Citizens' groups have continued to campaign against local development projects but the proposers have become more adept at using legislation and offers of compensation to frustrate their attempts.

One Japanese attribute which may explain the country's single-minded pursuit of economic success is the sense of group cohesiveness and loyalty to family, peer groups, business and the state. They remain strong forces in Japan, beginning in the home and reinforced at school, where the emphasis is on the cramming of facts. Individuality and any ideas for practical teaching are swamped by the pressure of crucial exams which begin as early as kindergarten. Teachers speak of the inflexibility of the curriculum which allows no room for nature walks. Spare time is filled with extra lessons or organized activities, leaving little leisure time for children to discover nature for themselves. Biology is on the curriculum but ecology rarely features; there is hardly any basic teaching about the inter-relationships between living organisms or how easily the balance can be upset. A survey conducted in 1983 revealed that over 70 per cent of teachers of science and social studies considered environmental education to mean teaching children to tidy their rooms and not drop litter.

Between school and becoming a 'salary man' (the term given to Japan's smart white-collar workforce) students have some chance to pursue individual interests. I was heartened by the story of some students who spent their summer holiday nights guarding a turtle rookery. A year later I met one of the leaders, now a dark-suited salary man living in another city; he did not know whether the turtles were still protected. In the all-embracing environment of a Japanese company where one typically works till seven or eight at night then socializes with one's colleagues until late, there is little opportunity to worry about such things. The pressures on businessmen are more acute than elsewhere because of the tradition of 'one company for life'. Should an individual complain about loss of wildlife or preach conservation he may well be branded as disloyal and unpatriotic. If he wants to hold a job down in a good company (it is extremely difficult to begin again) then he would be advised to keep quiet.

When I spoke to conservationists about hope for the future of the environmental movement the response was often gloomy or cynical, born of years of frustration. I was told more than once that the highpoint of the movement had been the pollution-conscious 1960s. In reality things are not quite so grim: because of difficult access to the high mountain ranges or distant islands some wild habitats survive and there are plenty of plants and animals worth fighting to conserve. And there are still pockets of resistance which need supporting.

The people of Shiraho, the fishing village in the Ryukyu Islands, for example, continue to protest against the airport which threatens their coral reef and their livelihood. In June 1980, the fishermen's cooperative (the umbrella body for the islands' fishermen) voted to relinquish the fishing rights over Shiraho reef in return for compensation. It was the first big political blow against the Shiraho fishermen and the beginning of a fight that has split the village.

Shiraho villagers campaigning against the airport which threatens their coral reef with slogans like 'Don't sell our sea'.

After an anti-airport demonstration in Ishigaki town Mrs Kuyama Oshima leads a prayer to the sacred rocks on Shiraho beach and speaks about the campaign. Like the wedded rocks at Ise, one is 'male' and the other 'female'.

I returned to Shiraho a year after my first visit to find that the villagers had organized a demonstration outside Ishigaki town hall where the Shiraho fishermen were due to take part in an important vote. Afterwards I drove back to Shiraho with one of the leaders of the demonstration, a lady in her eighties. She went straight to the sacred rocks on the beach, the site of the proposed airport, and spoke to them about how the fishermen had lost their vote that morning. To date the thirty fishermen of Shiraho have refused to accept any compensation. The remarkable side of the story is not the development itself but the fact that the villagers continue to challenge the need for the airport despite years of political pressure.

The widespread press coverage that Shiraho has received (the story has been featured on television many times) is drawing attention to the coastline. Yet, in Japan, of all countries, there is still no conservation body solely concerned with the protection of the sea. In the Ryukyus, whose turbulent history has fostered an independent spirit, some islands remain which have not yet been destroyed by grand harbours and other expansion schemes. Some of the islanders want to maintain their environment so that they at least can choose to use its resources in the traditional way. On Okinawa I met a young group who had started a business, screen-printing cloth using traditional dyes. They sold T-shirts displaying the rare wildlife of the island to publicize their conservation message. The bark of the Fukugi tree is extracted to dye cloth. When Dr Katherine Muzik, a marine biologist who has lived on the island for five years, protested that some three-hundred-year-old Fukugi trees had been unnecessarily cut down outside her home, she sparked off a tirade of anger against felling these trees which until then had lain dormant. All over Japan I came across people who cared about what was happening to their environment. Most were teachers, or photographers, students or naturalists. Some were scientists or journalists; housewives or priests.

It is an interesting time for the fledgling conservation movement. Each May in Tokyo hundreds of journalists and television crews wait in anticipation for a mother spot-billed duck to take her brood from her nest by an artificial pond across one of Tokyo's busiest roads to the Imperial Palace moat. Arguably the duck has become more of a media gimmick than a wild creature but the fascination with which her progress is monitored and the tenderness with which she is discussed speak for themselves.

The fact that industry is realizing that wildlife could become popular is another good sign. The lead was taken by the Suntory Whisky Company who in 1973 began their 'Save the Birds!' campaign. And professors, artists and media people help to bring credibility to the movement. Japan's favourite female television personality, Tetsuko Kuroyanagi, is an active supporter of the wildlife movement. In 1981 she wrote *Totto-chan*, the

The Okinawa rail, symbol of speed, runs along a T-shirt printed by a group of young people who have formed Project Core in an effort to encourage the use and conservation of the island's natural resources.

Fans of the spot-billed duck family at the Imperial Palace Moat, Tokyo. The moat is also home to little grebes, tufted duck and the occasional mandarin pair.

story of her days at an unconventional elementary school where the pupils went walking in search 'for the rhythms in nature'. The book became a bestseller and encouraged parents to take their children on nature walks. Although many people who care about wildlife do not think to join conservation groups, membership of the voluntary organizations has been growing. The Nature Conservation Society of Japan now has seven thousand members. (To put this in perspective, the British Royal Society for Nature Conservation has 165,000 members.) The Wild Bird Society of Japan with 17,000 members and 101 affiliated bird-watching groups, is the largest conservation body. Bird-watching has become increasingly popular in Japan and could be the forerunner of a powerful conservation movement. (The Royal Society for the Protection of Birds with over 500,000 members, just under 1 per cent of the population, is one of Britain's most powerful conservation lobbies while the American Audubon Society with 550,000 members, or 0.2 per cent of the population, plays a similar role.) The Japanese Wild Bird Society has perhaps the greatest opportunity of putting pressure on the government. In 1981 it opened Japan's first official wild bird sanctuary at Utonai in west Hokkaido, and since then four more have been created and many more are planned.

The Nature Conservation Society of Japan has concentrated on wildlife and habitats in immediate need of protection but it has also funded ecological research and worked to improve general knowledge about the state of the environment. A major campaign aims to protect the remaining large areas of primary northern beech forests. The forest of the Shirakami mountain range straddles the border between Aomori and Akita prefectures. At 45,000 hectares, it is the largest primary beech forest left in Japan and is home to a number of important species, including the golden eagle (*Aquila chrysaetos*), the goshawk (*Accipiter gentilis*) and the rare black woodpecker (*Dryocopus martius*). Much of the forest has already been eroded by a patchwork of commercial forestry plantations.

The Nature Conservation Society joined forces with World Wildlife Fund Japan and the Wild Bird Society to campaign for the forest. Environmental campaigns typically end in compromise

Oi bird sanctuary in Tokyo. In his booklet **Finding Birds in Japan, Tokyo area,** *Mark Brazil lists twelve birdwatching sites, two of which are sanctuaries.*

or failure but this time they have insisted on complete protection of the 16,000 hectares of forest which remain untouched. They have succeeded in holding up the completion of the road which would bisect this area and both sides are now waiting for the completion of environmental assessments of the potential impact of the road on the forest. The outcome of this battle is crucial to conservationists because Japan's officially fully protected five 'wilderness areas' range from only 370 to 1,900 hectares.

Mushroom cultivation in Kunisaki peninsula, Kyushu. Holes are drilled and spore placed inside the cut timber.

Meanwhile the campaign has generated interest in many smaller forest areas. The importance of forestry and its role in controlling and maintaining the flow of water is being recognized by bee keepers, salmon fishermen and even farmers and townspeople whose fields or homes have been flooded. A few local councils have bought small tracts of forest in order to protect them, if not for the wildlife then at least for the people. A National Trust was formed in 1974 based on the English organization, with the idea of buying small scenic areas to protect them from development. In its first decade, it moved slowly but in 1985 the tax laws were changed to encourage people to give money to the trust.

The three main wildlife conservation bodies have also joined forces to campaign for the Japanese serow. The serow has been protected as a 'special natural monument' since 1955 but foresters claim there are now too many. In 1979 the government decided to allow some shooting in areas where the serow was causing damage to the young cedar and cypress trees. Although permission is given to shoot around a thousand serows each year, mainly in Nagano and Gifu prefectures, some foresters remain dissatisfied. The government now proposes to degrade the serow's special status by nominating certain regions where the serow will be protected, yet allow hunting elsewhere. Conservationists maintain that many of the protected areas are above 1,800 m and that in the winter the snow will force the serows down to lower altitudes where they will face the guns. The government has also agreed to allow the sale of the serow's fur which, conservationists argue, will make shooting the serow an attractive proposition to hunters as well as genuine foresters.

In 1975 the Environment Agency estimated that there were about seventy thousand serows but their survey methods were criticized; how many serows there are and the damage they do is in dispute. It is possible that the serow's 'pruning' actually promotes growth. A group of volunteers, consisting mainly of students, has formed a society specifically to protect the serow. I joined them one Sunday in the mountains as they placed protective plastic nets over the main shoot of young cypress trees. They also daubed paint on the stems in order to compare the growth with that of unprotected plants. The volunteers have discussed the serow with foresters, some of whom, in Iwate prefecture, have said they would prefer to protect the trees rather than shoot the serows. Two-thirds of the volunteers had actually seen wild serows. They are convinced that if the Japanese came to value the serow they would accept that it needs somewhere to feed in winter.

Facing page: *A member of Kamoshika no kai, the group formed to promote protection of the serow, placing a plastic sock over a young cypress plant.*

The volunteers, like many other naturalists I met, were extremely keen to question me about the environmental situation in the West. They regretted the small number of conservation posts available in Japan and spoke of the challenges they faced: a powerful industrial lobby and general public indifference to the conservation of wildlife and habitats. Their problems brought home to me how relatively easy it is to be a conservationist in the West. The people were, however, heartened and not a little

A male yearling Japanese serow. In winter heavy snow forces the serows down to lower altitudes where they come into conflict with foresters. If government plans to remove the serow's protected status go ahead, conservationists say many more will be shot each year.

amazed to hear that conservation is far from satisfactory in Europe and America. Many of them had assumed that countries which so easily criticize Japan's protection of wildlife had got their own houses in order. Strong criticism and action from foreigners has sometimes ruined the progress that the Japanese have carefully but gradually made. In response to this some refuse to have anything to do with international conservationists. Many Japanese people still assert that westerners (even those who have spent many years in Japan) will never under-

stand them nor appreciate their way of working.

Some naturalists I met spoke of a Japanese way of looking after wildlife. I asked a teacher who was championing the case for nature walks in schools whether if, he were to see an eagle, for example, he would teach the children about food chains. But I was bringing western ideas into the conversation. 'Westerners', he said, 'put far too much emphasis on competition between species.' He would ask his pupils to watch the bird carefully and learn for themselves. They should draw the bird and only then go back and compare what they had discovered with what was written in the text books. A wildlife photographer who was making films to improve the knowledge and understanding of animals also spoke about the traditional Japanese harmony with nature. He felt that the way forward was to return to this way of living. In his opinion the Japanese crested ibis should not have suffered the indignity of being caged in the hope that it would breed in captivity and the red-crowned cranes should not be fed winter grain. They should be allowed to fly wild and free to fend for themselves, even if this means certain extinction.

Many Japanese point to western ways as being the cause of the world's ecological problems. The West's environmental conscience is young and, they say, the Japanese are still in the process of absorbing and assimilating the effects of industrialization. Many have not yet come to terms with the fact that instead of being passive participants they now have the power to determine nature's future. Instead of arguing the difference between East and West a few Japanese are simply keen to get on with the task of saving what they can.

It is certainly too late for Japan to solve her environmental problems solely by using technological solutions such as breaking down lethal chemical waste into less harmful products. Some consumer groups maintain that the situation will improve only when the people change their basic way of living and voluntarily give up their materialistic goals. Many Japanese businessmen recall working on the land when they were children. Many more remember the snub of defeat after the Second World War. For those who sweated to pull Japan out from her country roots and up from the disgrace of the war to the great economic power she is today, it is hard to accept that in the process much of their land was ruined. The poem at the beginning of this chapter questions the decision made in 1868 to follow the West into industrialization, abandoning many of Japan's traditional values. There is a general feeling that conservation may have a better chance of appealing to the young generation. A growing murmur of criticism is directed not so much at the state of wildlife and

The neon lights of Tokyo, the city which, according to many short-stay visitors, has not a blade of grass. Japanese who visited London after the Meiji restoration returned to Tokyo with the same impression.

habitats but at greed, at the over-dependence of the Japanese on consumer goods, at the increasing urbanization of life and the commercialization of so many arts and activities.

In each of the stories of the monkey, crane and turtle there is hope to be found. The Japanese have shown a special ability to sympathize with animals such as the Japanese macaque. People have begun to think of cranes as wild birds instead of as symbols and they have a real chance of helping the red-crowned crane to become a conservation success story. Towns like Hiwasa have shown that people prefer sea-creatures to be protected rather than hunted.

On a recent television programme in Britain, someone asked how the BBC could feature the Wild Bird Society of Japan's Crane Campaign when the country was still whaling. International criticism has prompted the introduction of some conservation laws and many Japanese conservationists welcome it for this reason. But they also fear that ungrounded criticism without due praise could lead to increasing nationalism and isolation, encouraging more exploitation of Japan's own wildlife resources. Conservation will only work in the long term if there is an internal change of heart. International recognition of the positive measures already taken must surely help. The conservationists who are fighting an uphill battle to save Japan and her wildlife need all the support they can get.

There is something in the heart of all peoples which objects to a dry, rational or scientific answer to everything and the Japanese with their instinctive awareness of beauty remind the whole world of the value of nature. And if they decide that Japan is reaching environmental crisis point history suggests that they could find the mental resolve to provide answers to the international problem of ecological abuse. Japan has demonstrated a remarkable ability to excel in whatever path she chooses to follow. The creative arts, design, industry, commercialization, consumerism and capitalism – she is master of them all. Her people have shown that they are prepared to renounce individual gain for the good of the group or the country. Over the years they have found pleasure in self discipline and frugality, satisfaction in the everyday and delight in the nuances and expressions of the natural world. The Japanese people have continually admired and praised nature's fertility, form, sadness and beauty, and they have recognized nature as an equal. These traditions could become the basis of conservation, for the many rather than the few. Today the Japanese have one of the worst reputations in the world for wildlife conservation but they could, if they chose, have the best.

JAPANESE HISTORICAL PERIODS

TO 1868

	PERIOD	DATE	EVENTS
STONE AGE AND ARCHAIC JAPAN	Pre–Jōmon	c.30,000 BC 8,000	Earliest datable traces of human habitation in Japan. Hunters and gatherers thrive in small settlements. Straw-rope-patterned earthenware used
	Jōmon	660 c.300	The official founding of the empire Rice cultivation begins. Clan units grow in power
	Yayoi	1st cent. AD 300	Emperor Jimmu reigns Yamato family gains supremacy
	Kofun	c.500	Yamato family founds the imperial line
CENTRALIZED CONTROL ESTABLISHED	Asuka	538	Buddhism introduced and adopted by the court. Court control strengthens over provincial clans
AGE OF THE COURTIERS	Nara	710 712	Nara established as capital. Chinese-inspired art and architecture flourish The *Kojiki*, Japan's first written history, compiled
	Heian	794 805 857 1007	Kyoto established as capital Saichō introduces Tendai sect. Heian courtiers, devoting themselves to art and luxury, fail to see the threat of increasing samurai power Fujiwara influence over court increases *Tale of Genji* written
	Kamakura	1185 1191 1192 1333	Minamoto clan establishes the first military government in Kamakura. Power passes from the court aristocracy to the warrior class Zen Buddhism introduced from China and Zen influence on the arts in Japan begins Minamoto no Yoritomo establishes Kamakura shogunate, a military dictatorship Emperor Daigo II tries and fails to re-establish imperial rule; Kamakura shogunate destroyed
AGE OF THE SHOGUNS	Muromachi	1338 1467–77 1542	Ashikaga Takauji establishes Muromachi shogunate The Onin War leads to nearly a century of civil strife First European contact with Japan made by Portuguese sailors
	Momoyama	1573 1582 1590 1600	Oda Nobunaga assumes control Oda Nobunaga assassinated Toyotomi Hideyoshi assumes control and crushes the remaining opposition ten years later The Battle of Sekigahara
	Edo	1603 1639 1853 1854–5 1867	Tokugawa Ieyasu establishes Tokugawa shogunate in Edo and begins a military rule that lasts for over 250 years National isolation policy enforced: Japanese are forbidden to leave the country. Dutch and Chinese traders only are allowed to visit one port, Nagasaki American naval officer, Commodore Matthew C. Perry, challenges Japan's isolation Japan concludes trading treaties with America, Britain, Russia, France and the Netherlands Tokugawa shogunate destroyed by conspiracy of western clans and imperial court nobles
BIRTH OF MODERN JAPAN	Meiji	1868	Emperor Meiji moves the imperial capital to Edo (home of the last shogunate) and renames it Tokyo; oversees an era of rapid modernization; abolishes the samurai-class ranking

ACKNOWLEDGMENTS

I am indebted to Naomi Kamei who escorted David Cobham, the director, and myself on film recces around Japan. She also organized and interpreted for Mike Herd and Mike Potts, specialist cameramen who filmed wildlife on five separate visits to Japan. And when she thought it was all nearly over because we were back in England and in post-production, she agreed to liaise with various experts in Japan and spent many disturbed evenings discussing points and checking information. And grateful thanks to Yukiko Shimahara who organized and guided the film unit through three sessions of filming people and places all over Japan. After a busy day's filming she was always ready to work late so that I could question someone further about wildlife or attitudes towards nature. Despite the impression given in the book, I was rarely alone while travelling around Japan. I was either with David, Naomi, Yukiko, or Simon McBride (whose wonderful photographs make this book) or the film crew, Chris Fryman, Junji Aoki and Hiroshi Yamashita, or Dr Mark Brazil, who introduced us to some of Japan's ornithological wonders, or Naoko Kakuta, Yuko Kikuchi, Akiko Oba, or Setsuko Yamazato. I am grateful to all of them for their helpful advice. Special mention for help both with sections of the films and with the book goes to Alfred Birnbaum, Dorothy Britton, Mie Haginaka, Tsuneo Hayashida, Professor Shizumu Hirose, Dr George Hlawatsch, Michael Huffman, Jonathan Holliman, Keigo Koyanagi, Miwako Kurosaka, Suehiro Matano, Dr Hiroyuki Masatomi, Yoshiki Mikame, Tom Milliken, Susumu Murata, Dr Katherine Muzik, Koji Nakamura, Reiko Nakamura, Mamoru Odajima, Professor Hiroaki Okada, Dr Stuart Picken, Keiko Sato, Toyoko Takahashi, Eishi Tokita, Dr Itaru Uchida and Sumio Yamamoto. And a thank you to the many other people who generously gave us their time and hospitality and did their best to answer questions.

Also thanks to the Cultural Agency, the Environment Agency, Friends of the Earth Japan, Japan Serow Conservation Group, Japan Whaling Association, Primate Research Institute Kyoto University, TRAFFIC Japan, World Wildlife Fund Japan, the Nature Conservation Society of Japan, the Wild Bird Society of Japan and the Yamashina Institute for Ornithology. I was given a multitude of ideas about attitudes to wildlife and conservation both by experts and by those discussing the subject for the first time. I cannot hope to have done justice to them all and in the scope of this book I have had to make many generalizations. I have also touched on a number of controversial subjects and it should in no way be inferred that the people whom I have mentioned necessarily agree with everything written or the final path I have taken.

I also owe thanks to various people in England who, in the final stages of the book, commented on sections or answered telephone queries: Brian Bocking, Geoffrey Bownas, Brian Groombridge, Richard Luxmoore, Dr Donald Macdonald, Stephanie Macdonald and Lawrence Smith; and thanks to the Ikebana Society, the International Crane Foundation, the International Whaling Commission, the Information Centre, Embassy of Japan, the School of Oriental and African Studies, the Natural History Museum and the Wildlife Trade Monitoring Unit.

A big thank you to Caroline Aitzemuller who supervised this checking and did some further research while I continued to write. Also many thanks to the Moving Picture Company who made the films possible, and the production team, Avie Littler, Gabi Kabza and Ruth Shepheard. And to Rainbird and their team, including Diana Levinson, Serena Dilnot, Lester Cheeseman and Cathy Blackie. The films would not have been made without David Cobham, who put faith in me to undertake this project, and was, as director of the films, constant companion and mentor in Japan. And thank you to Mike, my husband, who read the first draft, tolerated my long hours, and kept me going.

J. S-S

ILLUSTRATIONS

COLOUR
Anima Magazine: 86 above
Mark Brazil: 189 below
British Museum, London: 81, 98
Chester Beatty Library, Dublin: 97, 104, 147, 177
David Cobham: 30
Bruce Coleman, London (photo: Takana Kunio/Orion Press): 64
Masayuki Egawa: 63, 67, 73, 198
Choji Gima: 138 below
Hiroshi Hasegawa: 129
Tsuneo Hayashida: 116 below, 117, 118, 135, 143
Eiji Ishii: 20 below
Simon McBride: frontispiece, contents page, 6, 7, 11, 12, 14, 16, 17, 18, 19, 21, 22–3, 25, 28–9, 31 below, 32, 35, 37, 38, 39, 40, 41, 43, 45, 46, 47, 51, 52–3, 55, 57, 58, 60, 61 above, 69, 70, 72, 77, 80, 82, 84, 87, 88–9, 90, 92, 109, 110 above, 124, 126, 137, 139, 144–5, 146, 155, 156, 159, 161, 164, 170, 173, 174, 176, 178–9, 183, 189 above, 192, 193, 195, 196–7, 199, 200–1
Sydney L. Moss Ltd, London (photo: Derrick Witty): 186
Moving Picture Company Ltd, London: 123
Museum of Fine Arts, Massachusetts: 148
Mamoru Odajima: 74, 112
Rex Features, London (photo: Teiji Saga): 113
Tadashi Shimada: 111
Jo Stewart-Smith: 91
Taiji Whale Museum (photo: Simon McBride): 167

Eishi Tokita: 66, 68 below
Toyama Kinekan Foundation, Japan: 76
Dr Itaru Uchida: 149, 150, 151, 152, 154 above
Victoria and Albert Museum, London: 86 below, 95, 99, 105, 122, 128
Masahiro Wada: 114–15, 121, 141
Sumio Yamamoto: 26, 27

BLACK AND WHITE
Robert Harding Associates/Rainbird, London: 100–1
Kodansha Ltd, Tokyo (photo: Derrick Witty): 106
Kyoto News: 194
Simon McBride: 13, 34, 48–9, 50, 56, 59, 61 below, 68 above, 79, 85, 110 below, 120, 142, 154 below, 157, 162, 168, 180, 182, 184, 188, 191
Kinya Nakajima (photo: Simon McBride): 127
Tatsuo Nakazawa: 54
Mamoru Odajima: 31 above
School of Oriental and African Studies, London (photo: Derrick Witty): 102
Victoria and Albert Museum, London: 9, 103, 107, 116 above, 125
Wild Bird Society of Japan: 138 above
Takeshi Yamazaki: 20 above

ARTWORK
Bob Mathias: 10
Moving Picture Company Ltd, London: 132

TEXT

The author and publishers are grateful for permission to use the following material:

Chapter 1: 23, poem by Sakagamishi from *Monkey's Raincoat* by Lenore Mayhew (Charles E. Tuttle, Tokyo), 1985; 24, Ainu folktale adapted from *The Romance of the Bear God* by Shigeru Kayano (Taishukan Publishing Company, Tokyo); translations of names of Gods from *Japan, A Short Cultural History* by George B. Sansom (Stanford University Press, California)
Chapter 2: 53, 62, poem translations by Dr George Hlawatsch
Chapter 3: 89, poem translation by Paul Berry and Celeste Adams; 89, quotation from *The Narrow Road to the Deep North and other Travel Sketches* by Basho, translated by Nobuyuki Yuasa (Penguin

Classics), 1966; 93, 94 (above, centre), 95, poems from *The Penguin Book of Japanese Verse*, translated by Geoffrey Bownas and Anthony Thwaite (Penguin Poets), 1964; 94 (below), poem by Basho from *Monkey's Raincoat* by Lenore Mayhew (Charles E. Tuttle, Tokyo), 1985
Chapter 4: 115, poem translation by Dorothy Britton, from *The Japanese Crane – Bird of Happiness* by Dorothy Britton (Kodansha International, Tokyo); 124, poem translation by Dorothy Britton
Chapter 5: 145, poem translation by Dorothy Britton, from *National Parks of Japan* by Dorothy Britton and Mary Sutherland (Kodansha International, Tokyo)
Chapter 6: 179, 'The Lizard' by Hiroko Kagawa translated by Miwako Kurosawa and Alfred Birnbaum, from the original in *Hekiga* edited by Hagime Kojima (Sho-shin-sha, Tokyo)

Every effort has been made to trace the copyright owners of the material used in this book. The author and publishers apologise for any omissions and would be pleased to hear from those whom they were unable to trace.

INDEX

Numbers in *italics* refer to illustrations

INDEX